D1631835

The XJ-Series Jaguars

The XJ-Series Jaguars

A collector's guide
by Paul Skilleter

MOTOR RACING PUBLICATIONS LTD
Unit 6, The Pilton Estate, 46 Pitlake, Croydon CR0 3RY, England

ISBN 0 900549 84 X
First published 1984
Reprinted 1987

Copyright © Paul Skilleter and Motor Racing Publications Ltd

All right reserved. No part of this publication may be reproduced,
stored in a retrieval system, or transmitted, in any form or by any
means, electronic, mechanical, photocopying, recording or otherwise,
without the prior permission of Motor Racing Publications Ltd

Photosetting by Tek-Art Ltd, West Wickham, Kent
Printed in Great Britain by Adlard & Son Ltd, The Garden City Press,
Letchworth, Hertfordshire SG6 1JS

Contents

Introduction and acknowledgements

The XJ6 saloon has been Jaguar's most successful car ever; no other model over the years has surpassed it in numbers built or in technical excellence, and today – 16 years after its introduction – its production rate is higher than ever. Moreover, few if any luxury cars designed years later by rival manufacturers can yet match the XJ6 or XJ12 for their combination of performance and comfort – and none at all if price is also thrown into the equation. The XJ also represents the pinnacle of Sir William Lyons' own aspirations as a manufacturer of specialist cars, for the model which is shortly to replace it was designed and developed after his retirement.

It has often been said that Jaguar is in a class of its own; there are faster cars, there are more practical cars, but none looks like a Jaguar or drives like one. This uniqueness stretches right back to the original SS Jaguar of prewar days, through which – as Sir William himself wrote at about the time of the XJ6's announcement – 'a whole new approach to specialist cars' was started. 'Specialist' or, more recently, 'personal' cars now represent a very big sector of the market, but where previously the demand was met by a number of small specialist manufacturers, today the resources and flexibility of the mass-producers enable them to offer individually aligned cars through special models and a vast range of options.

Most of those specialist manufacturers have therefore perished, but Jaguar has survived, thanks to the company's ability to produce technically brilliant cars, superbly styled, in the right quantities to make them affordable. Certainly, thanks to the XJ's long production run, today it is more affordable than ever when the plentiful quantities of secondhand cars are taken into account. XJ ownership can begin for a few hundred pounds, and it is to assist anyone owning or thinking about buying an older XJ or XJ-S, as much as to record the XJ series' history, that this book has been written. Because the XJ is very definitely a car not just for historians, but one to be enjoyed for the superb road machine that it is!

In acknowledging the generous help I have received from many people in producing this book, firstly, I would like to record my thanks for a superb achievement to those who were responsible for the XJ series in the first place – Sir William Lyons and his engineering team of the period, which included Bill Heynes CBE, Bob Knight, Jim Randle, the late Malcolm Sayer, stylist Doug Thorpe and development driver Norman Dewis. Of those from the factory who helped me with this particular book, I would like to thank Doug Thorpe (again!), development engineer Paul Walker, Ian Luckett of the special facilities department, and David Boole's ever-helpful press and PR department, for much appreciated assistance on facts and figures.

I am also indebted to Chris Harvey for originally suggesting I undertake this title, and for supplying further pictures; Jim Patten of the Jaguar Driver's Club, for lots of information about running and old XJ; Ron Sotherton, also of the JDC and Jaguar parts manager at Premier Motors of Romford, whose knowledge and records were of enormous help in tracking down production changes; Roger Cook, for letting me photograph his XJ saloon under rebuild; and Graham Bigg, for a memorable day's drive in his superb Series 1 XJ12, which was a great help in refreshing my memory of the way early XJs perform. Andrew Whyte, undoubtedly the world's greatest Jaguar historian, assisted with pictures and advice, while I was very grateful to owners Peter Curtis (XJ coupe) and Brian Stead (XJ12 saloon), whose cars, along with the new XJ-S HE provided by Premier Motors of Romford, form the cover picture for this book.

The XJ6 series already has an unmatched reputation; if the reason for this has become clearer after you have read this book then it will have done its job!

PAUL SKILLETER

September 1984

6

CHAPTER 1

Ancestors and heritage

From Austin Swallow to Jaguar Mark X

Few manufacturers produce cars which set world standards, but Jaguar have done so on several occasions. The XJ6 was one of these, but there had been others before it, and to set the scene for this *Collector's Guide* we should first examine the XJ's ancestry and establish the extent to which this car evolved from the models which preceded it.

William Lyons set up business in Blackpool with his partner William Walmsley in 1922 and progressed from building sidecars to rebodying various small and medium-sized family saloons in the late 1920s. Easily the most numerous of the cars rebodied by the Swallow Coachbuilding Company was the Austin Seven; the first was completed in 1927, but full production did not begin until 1928, after Swallow had received an astonishingly large order for 500 of the type from Henlys, the London-based Austin distributors.

It was this order which prompted the move to larger premises in Coventry and provided the foundation for Lyons' and Walmsley's first car of their own – the SS 1. It is estimated that around 3,500 Austin Seven Swallows were built in all, and with their egg-shaped rear ends, cowled radiators and colourful (often two-tone) paintwork, they were very attractive and well-equipped little cars.

Again encouraged by Henlys, Swallow broke out of the purely coachbuilding role and next introduced an entirely new *marque*; the SS 1 and its smaller sister, the SS 2, arrived in 1931, examples which must have been little more than prototypes being displayed at the Olympia Motor Show in October. The larger car, especially, aroused no little comment at the show, mainly thanks to its styling – the use of a specially commissioned chassis had enabled the SS 1 coupe to be given a very low 'sports car' look, emphasized by an extremely long, multi-louvred bonnet. These styling features were up-to-the-minute and previously had been seen only on expensive, one-off Bentleys or suchlike cars. With the SS 1, Swallow made them available to thousands, for at £310 the car seemed incredibly cheap.

It was slightly unfortunate that the side-valve 16 or 20hp Standard engine which propelled the car didn't really possess the power to match these sporting looks, but the basic concept was right, and the SS 1 was developed into a very usable sporting coupe with a respectable 80mph-plus top speed. Tourer, drop-head coupe and 'Airline' styles supplemented the four-light saloon, and with a similarly improved SS 2, SS Cars Ltd (floated in 1934) had a comprehensive range of which offered style and a good measure of performance – at unbeatable prices.

Undoubtedly, the Austin Swallow and the SS 1 were the main reasons for Lyons' success up to 1935. But in that year a car of perhaps even greater significance arrived – the first Jaguar. This was the model name of a brand-new saloon from Foleshill, which attracted even more acclaim than the original SS 1 had in 1931, and this time without the blemish of sarcasm that some of the motoring establishment could not resist heaping on the SS 1 until the end of its days. Because unlike the earlier car, the Jaguar had a performance which fully lived up to its looks.

What made the SS Jaguar a truly serious proposition for the discerning motorist was its new engine; this produced over 100bhp, thanks to overhead valves, a new cylinder head having been developed by airflow tuning wizard Harry Weslake for the existing 20hp, 2,663cc Standard engine. The additional 30bhp

The name Jaguar arrived in 1935, carried by two stylish saloons. The 1½-litre shown here was sold virtually at cost to achieve volume sales and so reduce unit costs; many of its parts were shared by the similarly styled 2½-litre model.

gave the Jaguar a very useful performance advantage over the side-valve SS 1, top speed going up into the late 80s and the 0-60mph acceleration time reducing from 24 to 17.4 seconds. In the mid-1930s, these figures put the 2½-litre SS Jaguar firmly into the 'top 10' performance league in Britain, and at £395 it was almost ridiculously cheap. A 1½-litre 'baby sister' was even more astonishing value at £285.

The 1938 SS Jaguars which replaced the original wood-frame cars were bigger and better than their predecessors, the larger all-steel bodyshells being mounted on an entirely new, wider chassis frame with improved suspension. Also new was a 3½-litre ohv engine, while the 1½-litre model was given the 1,776cc ohv Standard engine. Mention should be made here, too, of the SS Jaguar 100, the sports car built in very small numbers using either the 2½ or 3½-litre ohv engine from 1936 to 1939, which did very well in rallies and added credibility to SS Cars' position as a manufacturer of sporting machinery. The 100mph 3½-litre

SS 100 certainly couldn't be laughed off as the original cycle-winged SS 1 might have been.

The success of the company prior to the Second World War was against all the odds. This was a period when specialist car manufacturers were getting ever deeper into financial problems, struggling against rising costs which were making their products prohibitively expensive, even for the well-off, and forcing a number of famous names into liquidation or takeover situations – Bentley, Sunbeam and Talbot among them. Bentley, even under the umbrella of Rolls-Royce, with its lucrative aero-engine division which more or less subsidized its car-manufacturing branch, failed to flourish, and an internal and secret cost comparison exercise against the contemporary Jaguar saloon could not justify the Bentley's higher price (double the Jaguar's), only 30% of which could be set down to superior design or materials.

The secret of Lyons' success lay not in cutting quality, in fact, but in efficiency and sound commonsense. Unfettered by a tradition which demanded the use of specially-made components throughout almost the entire car, as with Rolls-Royce, Lyons was able to buy-in components very cheaply and, indeed, the Standard Motor Company supplied most of the Jaguar's major chassis components from the engine downwards. Then, Lyons managed to achieve production levels which, although tiny compared to the mass-producers like Austin, Morris and Ford, were, at around 4,500 cars per year, three or four times more than Rolls/Bentley could achieve, and this reduced unit costs enormously by comparison.

The company entered the postwar years with a substantial reputation but – along with many other British manufacturers – an obsolete range of cars. War work had prevented the evolution of new models, though most car makers had managed to experiment with prototypes, especially during the last couple of years of hostilities. The prewar range (except for the SS 100) went back into production, therefore (but no longer with the SS prefix to its name) and a new Jaguar did not emerge from Coventry until 1948.

The unitary-construction 2.4-litre saloon can be nominated as the XJ's first **direct** ancestor; it was on this car that Jaguar developed the basic noise suppression techniques which were later applied with such brilliant success to the XJ6.

Like the S-type, the 420 was based on the Mark 2 saloons but had the same independent rear suspension as the E-type and Mark X; it was produced between 1966 and 1968.

That year, it was the XK 120 that captured all the limelight. The sleek two-seater was powered by an entirely new engine, a superb twin-cam unit designed by William Heynes and his tiny engineering team of Walter Hassan and Claude Baily. This had all the ingredients of a classic prewar Grand Prix racing engine, but none of the disadvantages – it proved to be tractable, quiet, reliable and requiring the minimum of tuning or maintenance. Yet it produced around 160bhp, about as much as the Americans were getting out of their best V8s of 5 litres or more.

The classic XK engine (so-called because it followed XJ prototypes, though these, of course, had no connection with the later saloon of that name), originally had a displacement of 3,442cc, and was to power every Jaguar made from 1952 until the V12 unit appeared in 1973, including the sports-racing C and D-type Jaguars which won at Le Mans in 1951, 1953, 1955, 1956 and 1957. It was originally designed for just one saloon, eventually to appear as the Mark VII.

The first Jaguar saloon to have a fully-tooled pressed-steel body (the Pressed Steel Company of Oxford, in fact, made it) and the first to be powered by the XK engine, the Mark VII replaced the interim pushrod-engined Mark V and lasted, effectively, until 1961, though it underwent minor changes during this period to become the Mark VIIM in 1954, the Mark VIII in 1956 and finally the 3.8-litre disc-braked Mark IX in 1958. This was definitely a landmark car in Jaguar's history, and no less than 46,537 of the four variants were made in total.

But while the Mark VII series might have represented the flagships of the Jaguar range in the 1950s, it was another, smaller car that was ultimately more significant and which can be nominated as the XJ saloon's direct ancestor. This was the 2.4 saloon, which made its bow in 1955 after a necessarily lengthy gestation period and was the first Jaguar with a body of unitary construction.

The Pressed Steel Company made the body, which was then delivered to the new factory at Browns Lane, Allesley, by road (as with the Mark VII). The engine was a new short-stroke, short-block version of the XK unit, its 2,483cc giving about 112bhp; the four-cylinder 2-litre edition of the XK unit, catalogued for the XK 120 in 1948, but never used, was initially earmarked for the new car, but was rejected, largely on the grounds of rationalization as the six-cylinder 2.4 unit shared many more parts with the existing 3.4 engine.

The new car posed fresh problems for Jaguar's engineers in that previous thinking on refinement (the suppression of engine and road noise and the transmission of vibrations and shocks) had to be substantially revised due to the entirely different characteristics of a unitary car compared to one having a chassis with a separate body mounted on top (like the Mark VII series). Because of the unitary shell's complex nature, with many box-sections interposed with large areas of unsupported steel sheet, all sorts of resonances could be set up by vibrations from the engine, transmission and suspension, and it was a major task to filter these out.

On the 2.4 it was done very successfully through the use of carefully chosen rubber and even spring mountings for the engine and drive-train; the rear suspension (an unusual arrangement whereby the live rear axle was suspended by quarter-elliptic leaf springs projecting from built-in chassis box-members under the rear seat pan) was mounted directly to the body, but at the front a large, heavy subframe was introduced to carry the front suspension, the frame being attached to the bodyshell by rubber mounts. Jaguar learnt much from the 2.4, knowledge which was to be put to good use in future models.

In 1957, the 2.4 was joined by the 3.4 litre, which of course was virtually the same car, but powered by the larger edition of the XK engine. An impressive 37,397 2.4s and 3.4s were built before they were replaced by the even more impressive Mark 2 range, which employed the same basic floorpan, but used all-new exterior panels. A third choice of engine – the 3,781cc unit first seen in the XK 150 and Mark IX – was provided, while thanks to a wider-track rear axle and altered front suspension geometry, handling was substantially better. The Mark 2 went on to become Jaguar's most successful saloon prior to the XJ series, over 100,000 being made in all, including Daimler derivatives. It also provided the basis for the 'independent rear' compacts, the 3.4-litre and 3.8-litre S-types of 1963 and the 420 of 1967 (which used the 4.2-litre engine also seen in the later E-types and Mark Xs).

The first Jaguar saloon to be independently sprung at the rear was, however, the aforementioned Mark X which arrived in 1961. This rather massive unitary-construction saloon was the true forerunner of the XJ and represented a big technical leap

The Mark X of 1961 was the biggest production Jaguar ever built and probably the widest British production car ever to be marketed. Directly preceding the XJ6, many of its features were adopted for the new saloon, including some of the basic styling traits – 'a Mark X with the air let out' is how the XJ is still described at the factory.

forward from the Mark VII/VIII/IX series. The car's most interesting feature was its rear suspension, which used the drive shafts as a suspension component along with forked, tubular lower arms and trailing radius arms; the whole was contained in a steel 'bridge' or subframe, which was mounted up under the bodyshell via rubber mountings to minimize the transmission of noise. Discs were inboard to reduce unsprung weight, and naturally discs were used at the front on a development of the Mark 1/2 subframe-mounted coil-sprung front suspension.

The Mark X was thus a very sophisticated car, and certainly the quietest, best-riding and quickest big Jaguar up to that time. But perhaps it was a little too big (it measured no less than 6ft 4in wide and 16ft 10in long – 1in and 5½in more, respectively, than the Mark IX) and too flamboyant to be a total success – in fact only a little over half as many Mark X and variants were made as Mark VII series models. Even the Americans found it not

entirely to their taste, which, as that country represented Jaguar's most important export market, was an undoubted disappointment to the company. But by way of consolation, the E-type, which shared the same rear suspension and engine, and the 3.8 Mark 2 were runaway successes in the United States.

The Mark X did teach Jaguar some valuable lessons, however, the principal one being that the prestige saloon of the range had reached, and indeed had passed, the optimum size. Previously, each successive model had been larger than the last, but no longer did 'bigger' necessarily mean 'better'. It was time to reconsider; the engineering of the Mark X series was basically right, and so now it was a case of encapsulating the science learned in a more compact and acceptable framework. The result, really the culmination of all William Lyons' efforts and enterprise since the original Austin Swallow of 1927, was the car this book is all about.

CHAPTER 2

The Series 1 XJ6

Setting a new standard

A completely new model from Jaguar is always an important event, and the arrival of the XJ6 in October 1968 was doubly so, for it heralded nothing less than a new set of world standards in luxury car design that were to endure for at least the next 16 years. That is not to say that the new Jaguar was flawless, or even innovatory – it was not; but it did bring a refinement, ride and handling package that was unequalled by any other car of the time. And, of course, it looked terrific.

How did Jaguar – a small concern in comparison with Mercedes, BMW and the builders of the Cadillac, General Motors – achieve so much with so few resources? The answer is not luck, intuition, or even simply the genius of one engineer, but rather slow, painstaking experimentation and development by a small, gifted engineering team which often had to compensate for budget limitations by sheer dedication and resolution. All, from Sir William Lyons downwards (he was knighted in 1956), were possessed of the perhaps unspoken resolve that Jaguar was special, that 'adequate' was never good enough for a Jaguar and that, regardless of the size and resources of the opposition, each new Jaguar had to be the best. They were not always successful in every design aspect, but with the XJ6 they came nearer to perfection than ever before.

Speed is not that difficult to achieve, and a good, dramatic shape is not the sole prerogative of the Browns Lane company – many worthy cars from both Europe and North America have proved that. But it was the overall refinement of the XJ6 that set it apart from its contemporaries, and the *manner* in which it covered the ground, accelerated and performed generally. This refinement, although present to a reasonable degree in prewar

Jaguars, had only really begun to establish itself as a hallmark of the make when Heynes brought his twin-cam engine and independent-front-suspension chassis together to produce the Mark VII; it was confirmed with the 2.4 unitary-construction saloon, which raised the technique of vibration and noise suppression to the level of a true science at Browns Lane.

Much was learnt from the 2.4, and the knowledge gained was applied to successive Jaguars with increasing success – the Mark X of 1961 might have been too big, but it was undeniably quiet and smooth-riding. Unfortunately, this most American of all Jaguars met with a very cool reception in that very country. Even its styling was given the thumbs down, and with Detroit turning towards razor edges and slab sides, the rotund Mark X was disparagingly likened to the 'step-down' Hudson of 1948 – and the similarity was undeniable. Nor was the handling particularly approved of, as most Jaguar drivers expected a crisper response to the helm than the Mark X could muster; 'a jelly on roller-skates' was how one disillusioned American owner put it.

So, as the time drew near for a Mark X replacement to be considered, its design parameters had already more or less defined themselves: the new car needed to be a little smaller, its styling had to break with what was really still the 2.4-litre shape much-inflated, and its handling and steering response had to be rather closer to those of the E-type than the aforementioned 'jelly'. Then there was Sir William's insistence on ever higher standards of refinement, and the necessity to regard heating and ventilation as fundamental design features, not add-on extras, as had tended to be the case with previous Jaguars – so important

XJ styling exercises began around 1964 with Sir William, as always, working with life-size mock-ups. Here the XJ roof and wingline are familiar, but the front has yet to undergo some changes. Sir William's home at Wappenbury was used to provide realism while viewing the protype bodies.

Although the car is still a two-door, the double headlamps have appeared and so has a more traditional grille in this later version. Wire wheels featured in XJ thinking until quite a late stage.

13

Almost there – the now-familiar chopped-off tail of the XJ6 in mock-up form. Sir William bends over to examine the front while to his right Fred Gardner, chief of the experimental bodyshop, looks on.

had they become to the customer of the 1960s, especially in North America.

Quite apart from the deficiencies of the Mark X (though in fairness one should say that it was not as bad as it is sometimes painted – bowling down the motorway at 110mph its appearance was dramatic and imposing, and no Jaguar since has approached its internal spaciousness), there were other problems for the new car to rectify; chiefly, these centred around Jaguar's model range which, by 1964 – the year in which serious work began on the XJ6 – had proliferated enormously. There was the Mark X, the E-type in coupe and roadster forms, the 2.4, 3.4, 3.8 and Daimler Mark 2s and the 3.4 and 3.8 S-types. These were a lot of models for a manufacturer only making 25,000 cars a year, and perhaps Jaguar's time-honoured policy of spreading the least amount of different components amongst the most cars was being taken a little too far.

The new car therefore needed to be far more than a direct replacement for the Mark X; rationalization was the name of the

game, and if the company were to maintain profits and continue to offer outstanding value for money, just one saloon car (albeit with various engine options) to be sold alongside the E-type seemed the way to go. The XJ6, therefore, was to replace all the earlier saloons; the last of the Mark 2 series, the slim-bumpered 240, was to depart in April 1969, though the Mark X (in updated 420G form) lingered on until June 1970.

How and why the XJ6 was such a quantum leap from these models in terms of refinement and overall excellence makes a fascinating story, and it begins with something as basic as the car's bodyshell. While Jaguar's engineers were not given an entirely clean sheet of paper when they came to design the XJ6, at least the body was to be entirely new and this allowed them to build-in certain features relating to refinement from the beginning.

In the automotive engineering sense, noise can be classified under three broad headings – structure-borne noise, airborne noise and wind noise. The first arrives in the form of vibrations

The XJ6 as we know it; a wide track, wide tyres and a low build all helped produce its superb, purposeful looks. Note the centre-bonnet raised moulding — originally a low-block 3-litre power unit was envisaged, but when the 4.2-litre engine was adopted instead the moulding had to be hurriedly incorporated.

The XJ6 was just as graceful from the rear, such was Jaguar's confidence, their name appeared nowhere on the car. Note the twin fuel filler caps and exhaust pipes protruding through the rear valance.

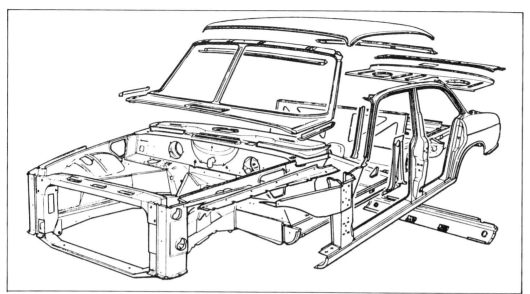

The main body structure of the XJ begins with the front diaphragm, travels back via the twin chassis legs/engine bay units to the double-skinned front bulkhead, then merges into the floorpan.

Below left, an interior view of the Series 1 bulkhead; also seen is the deep footwell and integral transmission tunnel. Below, boxed crossmembers, propeller shaft tunnel, very deep sills with an internal diaphragm, and wide-based centre door pillars all contribute to the shell's strength.

The XJ's rear suspension, developed from the Mark X's. The drive-shaft to the cast-alloy hub-carrier acts as the top component above a forked lower arm and twin spring/damper units are fitted. The suspension, inboard disc brakes and differential are carried by a bridge-type subframe which mounts via rubber blocks to the bodyshell.

The front suspension is carried on a box-section beam, viewed here from the rear. The top forged wishbone and bottom pressed wishbone/spring pan carry top and bottom ball-joints of a type used by Jaguar since the 1949 Mark V.

fed directly into the bodyshell by components attached to it – suspension, engine and transmission, exhaust system and so on. The steel shell absorbs these vibrations and then radiates them into the passenger compartment. The second is noise transmitted to the air by the working engine and suspension, picked up by the bodyshell and retransmitted to the occupants inside the car. Finally, wind noise is caused by the bodyshell rushing through the air and is mainly controlled by rubber seals.

The most significant amount of airborne noise generated emanates from the engine compartment – air intake roar, and the general mechanical 'thrash' of the engine and its ancilliaries. Obviously, the first line of defence against this noise is the front bulkhead or facia, and while in previous Jaguars Hardura-backed felt was used here, Jaguar found that what really cut down the transmission of this noise was double skinning of the metal bulkhead itself – such a bulkhead was five times more efficient than a single-thickness one in this respect. Double-skinning was thus incorporated in the XJ's bulkhead structure, the box-section resulting being utilized as a housing for the heater and (when fitted) the air-conditioning plant.

The remainder of the bodyshell broadly followed Mark X practice, the floorpans of both cars having two box-section cross-members, substantial box-section sills, ribbed floor pressings and very strong, triangulated centre door pillars. The Mark X was unusual in that its roof section was virtually unstressed, but because the XJ6 was lower, there wasn't room for massive Mark X-type sills and so the roof was made to contribute rather more to the strength of the shell – which, with a torsional rigidity of 8500lb ft/deg, was even better than the Mark X's already impressive 8000lb ft/deg. At 840lb 'in the white', the XJ6 bodyshell was lighter, too.

At both front and rear, box-section chassis legs took care of suspension and engine loads, the front legs being braced by the inner wing pressings plus a front cross-member, the rears by the double-skinned boot floor. The front wings and lower rear wing panels were bolted on, and 18 inches of controlled deformability

was built into the front of the bodyshell to meet crash-barrier requirements. Probably to avoid heavy tooling costs, the main inner structure was built up from a comparatively large number of smaller pressings, spot-welded together, which inevitably increased labour time and meant that there were many seams and joints to seal afterwards. The original XJ6 body was built at Pressed Steel Fisher's works at Oxford, and transported to Browns Lane unpainted.

When it came to turning that bodyshell into a real car, all Jaguar's unique expertise in the field of vehicle refinement was brought to bear. Head of the team which engineered the XJ6 was Robert J. Knight. Bob Knight joined Jaguar in 1945 after spending the war years as an aircraft power unit engineer with Armstrong-Siddeley and the Bristol Aeroplane Company, and quickly rose to become Chief Vehicle Development Engineer at Jaguar. Working under Bill Heynes, Chief Engineer, Knight was largely responsible for engineering the 2.4-litre Jaguar and, in doing so, pioneered many refinement techniques which were

The XJ's mechanical 'skeleton'; note the front transverse subframe mounts and the telescopic dampers which, alone of the suspension components, attach directly to the body. The considerable weight of the 4.2-litre XK engine also helps to damp out road shocks.

then applied to subsequent models – including, of course, the XJ6, and with brilliant effect.

The 2.4 taught Bob Knight that the complexity of a unitary bodyshell caused it to resonate at many different frequencies when excited by the inputs from engine, transmission and suspension units – 'structure-borne noise'. In cars with a separate chassis, like the Mark V and Mark VII, on which he had also worked, the ideal of preventing these vibrations from reaching the structure in which the occupants of the car were contained was much more easily achieved, as they could be damped out or retuned first by the rubber mountings of the suspension and engine on the chassis, and second by the mountings of the separate body on the chassis-frame. In a unitary car, this 'second chance' was absent, of course, and the inputs went straight into the passenger compartment.

The answer finally was, if you can't have one big separate chassis, then why not a couple of little ones? The effect would be largely the same. So the 2.4 was given a detachable front subframe, which carried the entire front suspension and was mounted to the body via very carefully designed rubber mountings. Then, when an independent rear suspension was brought in for the Mark X and E-type, this too was carried in a subframe. The results were excellent, and the idea was transferred in turn on to the XJ6 – Jaguar did toy with a directly-mounted rear suspension (which incorporated a torque tube on the differential housing instead of twin trailing links), but the same degree of insulation could not be achieved and the subframe idea was reverted to, despite the weight penalty.

As has been intimated, the design of the bushes which carried the subframes was crucial. At the rear, where the two pairs of coil-spring/damper units, inboard disc brakes and differential were all contained inside a pressed-steel 'bridge', they took the form of Metalastic V-shaped bonded-rubber blocks, two on each side inclined at an angle of 90 degrees. The positioning and resilience of these mountings were such that a controlled amount of rotation of the complete assembly was allowed (on an axis just forward of the differential axis), which on the Mark X had been discovered to be an important factor in damping out vibrations. The suspension's radius arms were the only components not contained within the subframe, and these were located under the body by circular rubber bushes.

Also like the Mark X, the front coil-spring/double-wishbone suspension was subframe-mounted, but here the frame's fabricated box-section construction was nearer to that of the compact Jaguars (the Mark 2 and its S-type and 420 derivatives) than the Mark X, which alone had been given a forged front subframe not unlike an old-fashioned beam axle in appearance. As with later Mark Xs, though, the XJ's subframe carried the front engine mounts as well as the suspension.

This was all part of the highly sophisticated front-end design which did so much to produce the XJ6's uncanny silence in operation. The basic subframe mountings were as for the Mark X; two 45-degree V-shaped rubber mountings, set 28¾in apart on the axis of the front wheels, carried the main weight of the assembly, while lateral forces were taken care of by bobbin-type rubber bushes set axially at the ends of box-member extensions projecting forwards from the main subframe.

However, there were a number of vital changes to the arrangement; probably most important, the yaw stiffness of the assembly was slightly reduced ('yaw' in this context is the swivelling movement of the suspension, when looked at from above, as road forces try to push the wheels backwards unequally on each side) to counteract the tendency of the new wide radial tyres to pick up extra road noise, while at the same time the yaw resonance frequency was reduced to about 13-14 cycles per second. This frequency was below that of most road inputs from the tyres, which simply means that the suspension was not made to vibrate and thus ultimately create noise in the bodyshell.

Additionally, or as a by-product, the compliance of the subframe-to-body mountings was increased by using high-hysteresis non-natural SBR rubber, and this effect in itself produced a useful reduction in the car's internal noise levels. A more visually obvious change was the relocation of the dampers; instead of being carried within the road springs, with their top mounting inside the suspension pillar, they were now attached directly to the body under the wheelarch. This enabled Jaguar to fit larger (Girling Monotube) units acting much further outboard on the suspension; thanks as well to carefully developed microcellular polyurethane mountings, this improved what is called the 'secondary ride', with shuddering effects being reduced at the front of the car.

The aluminium head of the XK engine, carrying its two chain-driven camshafts.

Ride qualities were enhanced over the Mark X as well; the new dampers contributed here, but the major improvement came from softer front springs. These were made possible because of the new anti-dive characteristics built into the front suspension – the upper wishbone mounting was inclined upwards at 3½ degrees to the horizontal, and the lower one downwards at 4 degrees. When the car was braked, this induced the kingpin to rotate slightly, the movement having the effect of jacking the body up and thus resisting dip by (in the case of the XJ6) 50%. As the springs could now be relieved of having to resist this, they could be derated by 25%. Also, Slipflex bushes replaced the previous rubber ones for the upper wishbone pivots, reducing the torque needed to rotate the arm to only 1lb/ft.

Besides carrying the suspension (including an anti-roll bar), the front subframe took some 80% of the engine weight; this had a double benefit – it further insulated the engine from the bodyshell, and the sheer mass of the engine helped cancel out road noise transmitted to the subframe by wheel bounce. The remainder of the engine/gearbox weight was taken by a single mounting at the rear end of the gearbox casing. This was rather special and had originally been developed for the 2.4; it comprised a very soft helical spring slung between two polyurethane bushes to take the small load imposed on it. This very low-rate mounting effectively counteracted an important source of engine vibrations in a car – those produced by the engine and gearbox bending as a unit about the bellhousing, which manifest themselves most strongly at the end of the gearbox.

It was thanks to all the thought and skill which had gone into the new car's engineering that Jaguar were able to use the beefy 205-section radial tyres which were such an essential part of the XJ's specification, contributing as they did to the car's impressive roadholding and to its looks. They had been developed specially for the XJ6 by Dunlop from their SP Sport range and were carried on 15in diameter steel wheels having 6in

20

rims – the widest seen up to that time on a production Jaguar. Less versed in chassis refinement techniques, Rolls-Royce for one had to persevere with quieter but less wear-resistant cross-ply tyres for some considerable time afterwards.

The XJ's steering was by Adwest Engineering and employed a rack-and-pinion for the first time on a Jaguar saloon; although a standard version of the 2.8-litre car was catalogued without it, power steering was in practice almost universal, keeping the number of turns lock-to-lock down to 3.3, yet with the minimum effort from the driver. A few police-specification cars were the exception. The rack was mounted on the rear of the front suspension subframe via Metalastic pads, and the universally-jointed steering column incorporated a Saginaw collapsible section.

Braking was by Girling, the front discs being gripped by a new three-pot caliper operating two smaller pads on the outside of the disc and one larger pad on the inside; this set-up was more fade and wear-resistant than the previous two-pot caliper arrangement. At the rear, the discs were inboard in usual Jaguar fashion with two pads each, plus a separate handbrake caliper.

The subject of power units for the XJ6 had been much discussed at the factory before the car was eventually launched with the choice of 4.2 and 2.8-litre engines. Complicating the issue was the parallel development of two V12 Jaguar engines, one an immensely powerful, four-cam unit designed with more than an eye on Le Mans, the other a 'softer', single-overhead-cam engine, which produced more torque low down but was not ultimately as powerful.

In the end, the lighter and less costly single-cam engine 'won', but neither it nor the possible V8 or straight-six variants were anywhere near ready when the time came to finalize the XJ saloon's design – all that could be done was to ensure that such a V12 would fit in the engine bay when the time eventually arrived. Until then, it was thought that a 3-litre version of the XK engine would suffice for all markets, this being a 2,997cc, 85 x 88mm unit based on Jaguar's existing 'short' block as used for the 2.4-litre engine. But even though it produced a creditable 185bhp, the all-important low speed torque was not there in sufficient measure, and at a fairly late stage in the XJ's development, recourse was made to the 4.2-litre engine as used in the Mark X/420G and E-type.

This used the 'staggered bore' linered block introduced in 1964 to replace the 3.8-litre unit in the E-type and Mark X, and of course it possessed all the XK engine's classic features – a massive seven-bearing crankshaft and an aluminium head containing twin chain-driven camshafts and hemispherical combustion chambers. Its rather long-stroke dimensions of 92.07 x 106mm were a little old-fashioned, and mitigated against high engine revolutions, but it had the immense advantage of being supremely well-proven. Every Jaguar built between 1952 and 1970 used one sort of XK engine or another.

For the XJ6, the 4.2-litre engine was used in two-carburettor form, rather than three as for the more powerful Mark X/420G and E-type; detail improvements included a larger impeller for the water pump and a modified cylinder head which dispensed with the water gallery, the water now circulating via transfer holes in the cylinder head gasket. The new cross-flow radiator was given a separate header tank to cope with the low bonnet line, and it was cooled at low speeds by a new 12-bladed fan on a Holset viscous coupling which disengaged at 2,500rpm. Previous cars had not always had a generous cooling capacity, and Jaguar wanted to increase the safety margin with the new car.

Having elected to use the 'big' XK engine, it now seemed prudent to offer a smaller unit as an alternative for those who wanted economy rather than speed, and so a long-stroke version of the 2.4 engine was developed. This 83 x 86mm, 2,791cc 'six' used the same straight-port head as its bigger brother, complete with two 2in SU HD8 carburettors, and it produced a quoted 180bhp gross at 6,000rpm against 245bhp at 5,500 rpm for the 4.2-litre unit (here it should be stated that at this period Jaguar's power output figures were somewhat inflated to match similarly optimistic claims from their American counterparts; nett installed bhp figures for these two engines were nearer 150 and 190). A further reason for the 2.8 unit was that it slotted in under the 2.88-litre tax bracket used in several European countries, including Germany.

Both engines were available with manual or automatic gearboxes, the former an improved version of the all-synchromesh four-speed unit introduced in 1964; it could be specified with or without a Laycock de Normanville overdrive. The automatic boxes were American-designed Borg-Warner

A six-cylinder engine installed. As it was designed with a V12 in mind, the XJ's engine compartment is reasonably spacious. The filler caps for the separate water header tank and power steering reservoir can be seen, as can the two SU carburettors, the damper top mounting points, the battery and the brake servo.

units, Type 35 for the 2.8-litre car, Model 8 for the 4.2-litre. Final-drive ratios varied according to which type of engine/ transmission combination was fitted, from 4.55 to 3.31:1 (see tables in the Appendices).

The interior of a Jaguar has always been a vital selling point, and the new XJ6 was sumptuously equipped in this respect. It went without saying that leather upholstery was used for the seat facings, and the reclining front seats were developed in conjunction with Slumberland for optimum comfort and support. High-quality vinyl door trims incorporated armrests and map pockets, there was thick pile carpeting, and rear seat passengers had their own heater vent. The dashboard was vintage Jaguar with big, black-faced speedometer and rev-counter set in walnut veneer above the steering column, and minor instructions and controls were positioned above the centre console. A basic-model 2.8 was catalogued with Ambla upholstery and no rear heater duct, centre armrest or rear door pockets, but few if any were produced.

Similarly, the appearance of a Jaguar has invariably been instrumental in its success, and where the Mark X failed to a certain extent, the XJ6 excelled. It was immediately hailed as one of the best-looking Jaguar saloons yet, long, low and with a marvellous body/wheel relationship thanks to the fat, low-profile Dunlop tyres. Yet in essence the Mark X shape was still to be seen, the new car retaining a sloping-forward radiator shell and fairly rounded sides. Indeed, Jim Randle, Jaguar's Product Engineering Director, has described the XJ as 'a Mark X with the air let out'. Praise for the car's body design was worldwide, and came not just from customers and dealers, but also from car designers and similar professionals.

If the car looked good, it performed even better, and those who were fortunate enough to drive one in those early days knew after even a couple of hundred yards or so that here was a car which represented a quantum leap in standards of refinement and handling. Even today, an XJ saloon is an immensely impressive car, so the effect on a driver used to the standards of the late 1960s can be appreciated. No wonder that the first road tests of the car produced rapturous, almost awe-struck passages of prose in British motoring journals: 'If Jaguar were to double the price of the XJ6 and bill it as the best car in the world, we would be right there behind them', stated *Autocar* boldly, after a

Inside the XJ, Jaguar had remained surprisingly true to tradition – wood veneer and leather were expected, but perhaps not the centrally-placed secondary instruments and rocker switches (only the indicators were stalk-controlled, and the overdrive when fitted was operated by a switch on the gear-lever knob).

An enterprising feature for rear-seat passengers is their own heater outlet; the snag is that ash can be blown everywhere if the ashtray is used at the same time!

1,300-mile test which included Bank Holiday traffic and high-speed work on the Continent. They reckoned the XJ6 to be smoother and quieter than the Rolls-Royce or the Mercedes-Benz 600, and with better handling than the E-type.

Motor also published its test in the spring of 1969, having sampled a manual/overdrive car as opposed to *Autocar*'s automatic version, and were similarly enthusiastic: 'We believe that in its behaviour it gets closer to overall perfection than any other luxury car we have yet tested, regardless of price.' It was no coincidence that the word 'uncanny' cropped up in both road tests when the ride over rough surfaces was discussed. *Motor* added: 'The resilience is there, but none of the wallowy swell.'

Both journals praised the car's silence, its 100mph cruising speed inducing 'no wind whistle, no engine noise, no road roar and no transmission whine', according to *Autocar*. As for outright performance, their automatic car gave 120mph and 0-60mph in 10.1 seconds, while *Motor's* overdrive example managed 124mph and reached 60mph in a rapid 8.8 seconds (by way of comparison, the automatic-only Rolls-Royce Silver Shadow of the period had a top speed of 115mph and a

The rear of the Series 1 cars is beautifully trimmed but — compared to Mercedes-Benz and Rolls-Royce equivalents — only adequate legroom is provided.

This is the interior of that rarity, the 'standard' model 2.8-litre. Note the absence of a lid for the centre glove box and the lack of map pockets in the doors. Ambla instead of leather upholstery was used for this model.

0-60mph time of just over 10 seconds). Fuel consumption wasn't such a debating point in those days, and the XJ's 15.3mpg (virtually the same for both automatic and manual cars) passed without serious criticism, *Motor* pointing out that economy-minded owners would probably get approaching 20mpg with gentle driving.

The Daimler Sovereign of identical mechanical specification came along in October 1969 and was also offered in either 2.8 or 4.2-litre forms. Bonnet and bootlid chromework distinguished the cars externally, plus the 'D' instead of a leaping jaguar on the side of the front wing.

As for the 2.8-litre car, Jaguar deliberately refrained from lending an example for a full road test in the UK, perhaps because initially it was thought that sales of this model would be concentrated overseas, or possibly because Jaguar wanted the 'flagship' 4.2-litre's performance figures to be uppermost in people's minds. In fact, considering the weight of the XJ6 (around 33cwt) the 2.8-litre didn't perform badly, factory figures taken at MIRA (the motor industry's test ground at Lindley, not too far from Coventry) showing that it could achieve 117mph and 0-60mph in 11 seconds in manual gearbox form, the automatic being a little slower at 113mph and 12.6 seconds. Fuel consumption could be kept at or above the 20mpg mark, though it would drop to 15 or 16mpg if the car was driven hard.

The nearly 'over-square' dimensions of the 2.8-litre made it a

very free-revving unit which would quickly and willingly reach the 6,000rpm red band through the gears – in fact, when driving a manual 2.8 car briskly, it's essential to keep an eye on that instrument to avoid over-revving, and at high revolutions it was certainly a sweeter engine than the 4.2, which tended to become a little 'thrashy' above 4,500rpm. The reduced performance available was most noticeable when accelerating in top gear from fairly low speeds (40-60mph took 8.7 seconds as opposed to the 4.2's 6.4), and at high speeds, when, of course, the response to full throttle at, say, 90mph was much less impressive than with the larger-engined car. But the 2.8-litre was by no means underpowered, and its comparative lack of success was probably due to other factors.

One aspect of the XJ6 which hasn't yet been touched upon was its value for money. Always a Jaguar attribute, the new XJ

Inside, the Soveriegn is identified by wide-pleated, non-vented leather upholstery and contrasting door trim.

Despite having the best heating/ventilation system of any Jaguar up to that time, overseas owners soon complained of poor fresh-air throughput; this was partially countered in 1970 by adapting the headlamp peaks to act as air intakes. Inside, the air was ducted to the footwells and controlled by a push-pull lever.

was no exception to a rule which Lyons established from the very first SS 1. The manual/overdrive 4.2 saloon retailed at £2,314 in 1968, or a mere £44 more than a top-of-the-range Rover (the slower and less refined 3.5 coupe), while if you plumped for a 2.8 you'd actually *save* £300! When it came to comparing the XJ6 with other true prestige cars, the Mercedes-Benz 300SEL sold for no less than £5,624 in the UK, and the current Rolls-Royce would have set you back over £7,000.

The upshot was that there immediately developed a long waiting list for the new Jaguar, despite the fact that initially the car was not exported to the United States (then Jaguar's most important overseas market). Eighteen months or even two years delivery were being quoted by dealers, and small-ads in the London evening papers offering 'delivery mileage' new cars at a considerable premium over list became relatively common.

It didn't help that production of the XJ at Browns Lane was slow to get under way, just about 8,000 being made in the first

A number of XJ6s were produced to 'police' specification with stiffer rear springs to improve the load-carrying capacity, and sometimes they were supplied without power steering.

12 months, and while that figure was more than doubled during 1970, an estimated 5,000 cars were lost due to a piece-rate dispute at Pressed Steel Fisher. Nevertheless, 30,000 Jaguars of all types left the factory during that model year, XJ saloons accounting for two-thirds of that record figure. Then, in 1971, overall production was hoisted to 32,589, of which 23,546 were XJ6s and 5,158 were Daimler Sovereigns. The XJ saloon was now easily established as Jaguar's best-selling model ever on an annual basis, and that 1971 total (which included E-types) constituted a record for Jaguar which would take a long time to be beaten.

The Daimler Sovereign version of the XJ had come along in October 1969, a couple of months after the first car to bear the name had ceased production – this had been the Daimler version of the Jaguar 420 saloon, essentially an updated S-type with a Mark X-type front and powered by a twin-carburettor version of the 4.2-litre engine. It had arrived in 1966, helping to extract a bit more life from S-type tooling and filling in before the arrival of the all-new XJ6.

The new Sovereign was simple badge engineering and was identical to the XJ6 apart from its fluted Daimler grille and badging, and the incorporation of a number of 'extras' as standard, such as overdrive on the few manual versions made. Both 2.8 and 4.2-litre engines were used. So now, with the dropping of the old S-type-based 420 models, Jaguar had put all its eggs irrevocably in the XJ basket, and while the XJ was usefully smaller than the Mark X/420G, it still couldn't be labelled a 'compact' car. In the relatively prosperous years of the late 1960s and early 1970s this didn't seem to matter, but later on, in the fuel-conscious post-1973 oil crisis world, the lack of a downsized model was to become more acutely felt, but neither the will nor the resources were then available to tackle the problem of a model range which had gone from the overly extravagant to the dangerously narrow in the space of two or three years. Only in the mid-1980s is another 'compact' Jaguar model range being planned.

Export has always been a major consideration for Jaguar, and over the years the company has been one of the largest dollar-earners for Britain. Looks, performance and 'Old English' comforts sold the car abroad, mainly – but not always – to enthusiast types who fell in love with the styling and liked running a 'different' (*i.e.* European) car. In North America, the XJ lived up to the expectations set successively by the XK sports cars, the Mark VII, the 3.4/3.8 saloons and the E-type. It has to be said, however, that Americans had long maintained a love-hate relationship with Jaguar, the British cars having failed to match the reliability of the home-built product – which, for all its faults (like cumbersome handling, often appalling brakes, and an inordinate thirst for fuel), would just keep going with the very minimum of attention. Nor did the Jaguar always have the same standards of ventilation and heating as even low-priced American sedans.

So not all aspects of the 4.2 automatic tested by *Road & Track* magazine in 1972 brought forth unqualified praise: 'The car is antique in certain ways, sometimes amusingly and sometimes irritatingly so. In other ways it's as modern as a production car can be.' So while the car was rated as 'one of the best-riding cars money can buy', with 'delightful handling', which was better than its Mercedes or BMW rivals, the XK engine was reckoned to be 'just below the general quality level of the car', getting 'rough and noisy' above 3,500rpm. The heating and ventilation system *still* fell short of the best modern practice (with the optional $549 air-conditioning plant not able to provide the output of domestic cars), and the array of lookalike rocker switches were labelled 'archaic'. Surprisingly, the brakes weren't very impressive, with stopping distances being long, and evidence of slight fade.

'A strange and wondrous car, this XJ6', summed up *R&T* 'It's one of the most beautiful sedans in the world, and certainly one of the best-handling and best-riding ones . . . But in some respects – rather important ones – it seems to have been designed in a vacuum; it's as though the designers refused to look around them and see what everyone else is doing these days. Is it British pride, or simply British insularity, that lies behind the XJ6's ergonomic backwardness? The XJ is a good car, make no mistake, but it's maddeningly short of what it could be if it were designed as competently all the way through as its suspension and exterior bodywork are.'

The reasons for these peripheral shortcomings were, perhaps, symptomatic of Jaguar's small size – then as now they were a tiny company compared to (say) Mercedes, with less than a tenth of that company's annual output, and they were similarly dwarfed by the even larger North American car makers. There was thus less money and facilities available for development, and (a mixed blessing this) less people involved internally to observe what the world was doing and to criticize the product. But there was no complacency at Browns Lane, and such observations were evaluated and – as we shall see – generally acted upon.

Similarly, European road tests of the XJ6 tended to be less euphoric than British ones, though the superiority of its ride and its general refinement were usually acknowledged as putting the car in a class of its own; also, a certain lack of space inside was becoming noticeable, a point taken up by the motoring press as home, as well.

But reliability is also a key factor when evaluating a car, and here the XJ6 of the 1970s did not fare particularly well. Production levels might be running at an all-time high for the company, but somehow quality was not being maintained – and in a complex modern car like the XJ6 there was a lot more to go wrong or come adrift. Rarely was the car's basic engineering at fault, however – the few items which can be cited under this heading are the already-known tendency of the differential seals to deteriorate under heat from the inboard discs and leak oil over the brakes, and the propensity of the 4.2-litre block to crack between bores at the top if a drop in coolant level had induced overheating. No, the real problems lay in build quality, and poor design or manufacture of ancillary equipment by outside contractors, and these factors dogged the XJ range for a number of years.

Like every other manufacturer, of course, the XJ was subjected to a continuing programme of improvement as weaknesses came to light under operational conditions and as the engineering department evolved better ways of doing

One of the last Series 1 saloons. The few changes from the original specification visible here are the outward-curved exhaust pipes, the revised bootlid chrome and the larger reversing lights made possible by transferring the reflectors to below the rear lights.

things. A comprehensive list of these production changes can be found in an Appendix, but it's worth mentioning a few of the major examples here. Petrol fumes had been a common complaint from owners of early cars, and new filler caps incorporating anti-surge flaps were soon brought in, while redesigned (SU HS8) carburettors with a new automatic enrichment device arrived in March 1971. Tyre clearances at the front were sometimes marginal under certain conditions and new spring pans and, finally, modified wheelarches were specified. The front seats were given provision for head restraints in August 1969 and, in 1970, rather feeble fresh-air intakes were installed in the footwells, mainly at the behest of overseas owners. A small-scale revision of the dash took place in the spring of that year, with non-reflective bezels being fitted to the instruments, but a more significant improvement on the 4.2-litre car was the adoption of the Borg-Warner Model 12 automatic transmission in place of the Model 8, with its better override control and more responsive behaviour. Final-drive

Automatic version of the XJ6, with hefty 'T'-handled selector on console otherwise much the same as the manual. Steering column on all cars was adjustable in-and-out but not for rake.

ratios were raised to give less stressful high-speed running and slightly better economy, too.

But much more fundamental changes were on the way, and even the original launch publicity had hinted at new and exciting power units which were to be made available for the XJ saloons. So when a superb, all-alloy V12 engine of 5 3 litres appeared in the E-type for 1971, everyone knew what was in store for Jaguar's four-seater – and with the promise of immense power and torque, combined with a standard of ride and handling that had already become a legend, it did indeed seem apparent that the world's best car would shortly be announced . . .

CHAPTER 3

The Series 1 XJ12

A racing engine changes course

Thinking at Jaguar about a V12 engine goes right back to 1955, when the factory was in the middle of its highly successful Le Mans programme – the D-type had won that year, and would for the next two years running, but William Heynes knew that the faithful XK engine's development potential was nearly exhausted. Compared with Ferrari and Maserati it was already down on power, the car obtaining its results on reliability more than anything else, and the gap could only widen in the future. If Le Mans was to continue as an objective into the next decade, a completely new engine would be required, and so, under the direction of Heynes, power units engineer Claude Baily drafted out an over-square 5-litre V12 which would be capable of supplying the additional horses. But in 1956 came Jaguar's withdrawal from racing and the project was sidelined.

It was taken up again in the early 1960s, when once more Le Mans exerted its appeal, and this time a number of 'real' engines resulted, massive four-cam units which visually looked like two XK heads on a single block. Power was the major objective, and while the engine was scheduled for use in Jaguar's road car range eventually, its suitability for racing was a major part of the design team's brief. It first ran in August 1964, and produced about 500bhp at 7,500rpm, even in a fairly mild state of tune.

Then, early in 1966, the V12 met the new sports-racing car Jaguar had built for it – the XJ13. This sleek, mid-engined projectile could have formed the basis of a Jaguar works team for the 1966 or 1967 Le Mans events, but once again the climate of opinion within Browns Lane changed, largely due to the company's amalgamation with BMC that year, and the XJ13 never turned a wheel in anger – indeed, its very existence was kept secret until 1973.

Back in the mid-1960s though, doubts were creeping in as to whether such an engine was really suitable for a production Jaguar – it gave ample power, to be sure, but at rather high rpm, and the four-cam configuration made the engine both bulky and expensive. It was at about this time that Walter Hassan and Harry Mundy joined (in the case of Hassan, rejoined) Jaguar from Coventry Climax, where they had been instrumental in the design and development of the engines which had powered British Formula One cars to four World Championships within nine years. Hassan in particular felt that the 'racing' approach to Jaguar's new power unit was not the correct one, and he strongly favoured an alternative engine which was being developed in parallel.

This was still a V12, a cylinder configuration which was still favoured because of the inherent smoothness of such an engine, and because it would have enormous prestige value – at that time only the most exotic road cars could boast of 12 cylinders. The cheaper option of a V8 was ruled out, largely due to the fact that almost every car built in the United States was powered by such, and Jaguar wanted to establish exclusivity. The design of the engine, under the watchful eye of Heynes, was shared by Hassan, Mundy and Claude Baily, who with the first two had been part of the original XK engine design team.

This second engine was very different from the first, and flew in the face of tradition for a Jaguar power unit – gone were hemispherical combustion chambers and twin overhead camshafts per bank, for instance. The chamber was now almost entirely in the piston, a 'flat' cylinder head being used. This had

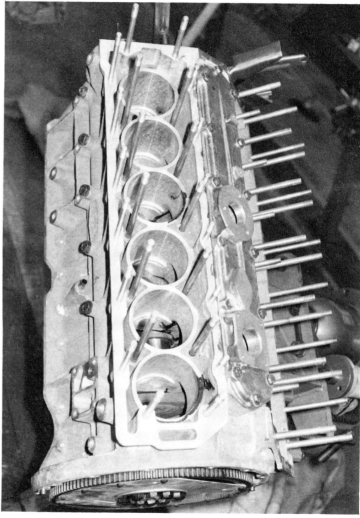

Jaguar's original 4,991cc V12 engine (top left) used classic XK features like hemispherical combustion chambers and twin overhead camshafts; it produced around 500bhp, even in road-car trim, but would have been difficult to fit in the XJ's engine bay. The eventual production V12 (above left), strongly advocated by Walter Hassan in particular, was a much simpler design with one camshaft per cylinder bank. Note the central distributor and Zenith-Stromberg carburettors on this early example. For the first time, a production Jaguar engine was given an aluminium block; cylinders were set at an angle of 60 degrees and the engine was built on extensive new tooling at the old Daimler factory at Radford.

The V12 engine installed in the XJ saloon; 11in induction pipes take the mixture from the carburettors to the inlet ports and water, fuel and electrical lines add to the confusion. The 'capstan' throttle arrangement gave a beautifully progressive movement, but the big air cleaners were only partially successful in subduing intake roar at high revs.

Underbonnet temperatures were a cause of concern and the fan-cooled battery (below) was much commented on at the time and later fitted to six-cylinder cars. In fact the electric fan rarely cut-in. The V12 Jaguars carried ventilated discs (another feature to be commonized later) and uprated springs to cope with the additional 80lb over the front wheels.

The original XJ12. External changes were few, but instantly recognizable from the front, with a simple, vertically-slatted grille replacing the less pleasing 'grid' version used on the XJ6. A discreet 'V' symbol is displayed on the central bar.

Little to distinguish the bigger-engined car from the side, though the ventilated wheels were fitted as standard (and made an option for the six-cylinder cars).

Overseas, the XJ12 was an even more exclusive car. This one is being used as a course car for the 1973 Le Mans 24-hour race; though 11 years were to elapse before a Jaguar appeared again in that race, when it did so it was powered by basically the same V12 engine.

been developed from first principles and was chosen because of the extremely good power and torque outputs it gave in the lower and middle (up to 4,500rpm) speed ranges – which is where it counts in a road car. It also had the great advantage of being relatively simple and cheap to cast and machine.

Single overhead camshafts per bank were adopted for basically similar reasons – simplicity and cheapness. Twin cams per bank would have demanded a far more complex drive, and there was the secondary advantage that a shorter engine (and hence a lower bonnet line) resulted from the single-cam approach. Interestingly, Jaguar rejected the increasingly fashionable belts for turning the cams and stayed with a single-stage chain drive; not only did they have a vast experience of them, but a chain had the advantage of being narrow (the engine was getting quite long enough as it was!) and could drive ancilliary components from both sides.

The remainder of the engine was up-to-the-minute, having an aluminium crankcase (incorporating a 4-inch 'skirt' beneath the crankshaft line to increase its rigidity) and of course aluminium cylinder heads. Its dimensions were very 'over-square', with a

bore and stroke of 90 x 70mm, giving a capacity of 5,343cc; breathing was via four Stromberg 175 CD carburettors on the end of long inlet tracts either side of the 'V' – a fuel-injection system had been considered, but its development had been postponed by the manufacturers (Brico), while no suitable British downdraught carburettors (which would have been contained within the 'V') were available. The entirely new Lucas transistorized ignition system used a single distributor sitting within the 'V'.

Before the engine was cleared for production, however, there was one more hurdle to be overcome. The net horsepower figure was 265, but this was some 30bhp down on what the four-cam 5-litre was producing, and Heynes in particular tended to favour the latter engine despite its complexity. The matter was only resolved when two Mark Xs were matched against each other, one powered by the flat-head V12 and the other by the four-cam 'hemi'. While the four-cam car was ultimately the faster, the flat-head Mark X scored heavily on acceleration from low and medium rates of rpm; that clinched it, and the all-alloy 5.3-litre flat-head was given the go-ahead for production.

35

The interior of the XJ12 was still basically as for the XJ6, but on the centre console black-grained vinyl replaced the bright aluminium and a 'V12' badge was added. Electric windows on all models so equipped are controlled by switches on the face of the centre glove box.

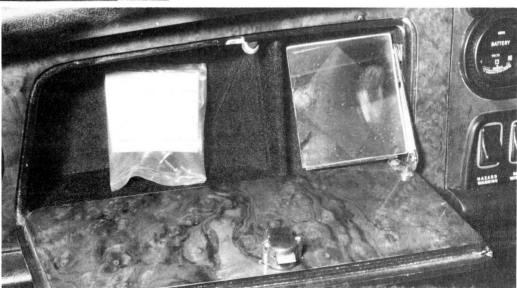

Like the XK engine before it, though, the new power unit wasn't seen in a Jaguar saloon until it had been given a trial run in a sports car, in this case the E-type, which was released in revised Series 3 form with the V12 engine during March 1971. This enabled the engine plant at the old Daimler factory at Radford to sort out any teething problems with both the engine and its production line (which had cost some £3 million to install) before anything like a high volume was required.

So the XJ12 did not appear until July 1972, possibly a little behind schedule due to the complexities of installing the new engine, even though the car had been designed with a 'V' configuration power unit in mind from the start. The engine itself slotted in reasonably well, but it was squeezing in the various ancillary components all around it that caused the headaches, and Jaguar's production engineers were heartily glad that the four-cam unit hadn't in the end been chosen.

The next problem was that of heat; an engine of this size generates a lot of it, and bonnet louvres were hardly appropriate for a Jaguar saloon. So the battery was given its own electric cooling fan (which cut in on the rare occasions when the

The original XJ12s have manual chokes controlled by a nicely engineered slide lever set above the bonnet release. Note the 160mph speedometer, matched by a 7,000rpm rev-counter.

Typical Jaguar detail – the vanity mirror set into the glove compartment. The plastic bag contains a cigarette lighter plug for running an inspection light.

temperature became excessive), while the actual cooling of the engine was undertaken by a horizontally divided crossflow radiator with separate header tank. The 4-gallon capacity radiator incorporated a transmission oil heat-exchanger, and forced air was supplied by a 17-inch engine-driven fan (with a viscous coupling that allowed slip above 1,700rpm) backed up by a thermostatically controlled electric fan. Engine oil was cooled by a twin-tube oil cooler mounted below the radiator (as opposed to being built into the sump as on the Series 3 E-type). Stainless-steel shields protected the engine and steering rack mountings from exhaust manifold heat (these could glow red hot on North American cars, which had air injection), and the exhaust downpipes were double-skinned to reduce noise.

While the V12 E-type had been available with either automatic or manual transmission, only the former was offered for the saloon; this was the Borg-Warner Model 12 box, suitably re-engineered by Jaguar to take the extra torque and revs of the new engine. While a few enthusiasts regretted the lack of a manual gearbox, the automatic was really more appropriate for a luxury saloon and it's unlikely that many cars would have been

The XJ's wide, deep, but quite shallow boot area demonstrated by a 1972 XJ12; petrol tanks are concealed in the rear wings on each side, the spare wheel being in a square compartment under the floor. The tools and jack are as supplied new.

The author was able to verify the original XJ12's performance at the time; here is the car at an indicated 141mph and still accelerating (the rev-counter shows 5,300rpm). The same car achieved 60mph in 7.3 seconds and 100mph in 19.1 seconds.

The XJ has been described as a uniquely British blending of the modern with the antique – so this picture taken in October 1972 of the XJ12 tested by the author has a fitting background in the shape of an 18th century lodge.

ordered without it.

In its new guise, the car was altered very little from the familiar six-cylinder version which, of course, continued in production. The V12 engine, at 680lb, weighed a modest 80lb more than the 'six', altering the car's weight distribution from 52.8/47.2% to 53.8/46.2% front to rear, the increase over the front wheels being met by slightly stiffer front road springs. Slowing such a powerful and comparatively heavy (35cwt) car also brought an uprating of the brakes, ventilated discs being installed on the XJ12 (some while later these were standardized over the range). A reinforced version of the Dunlop 205-section tyres was specified, though the rim width stayed at 6 inches. The final-drive ratio was 3.31:1 and a Powr-Lok differential was standard at this time.

The traditional XJ6-type interior was retained, though the driver now faced a 7,000rpm rev-counter and had to operate a nicely-engineered manual choke lever situated under the dash.

Externally, the changes were equally discreet, manifested by a new and simpler radiator grille with vertical slats and a slim 'V12' badge in black and gold, and 'XJ12' script on the bootlid – though, at last, the word 'Jaguar' appeared here, on the other side of the lid.

The poor XJ12 seemed to have been ill-fated from the start. A rare strike at Browns Lane during the month of its announcement prevented its release for a short while, and then, in 1973, the world was hit by the so-called 'energy crisis', with an artificial oil shortage suddenly making even drivers in the new-Jaguar bracket fuel-consumption conscious. Herein lay the XJ12's Achilles' heel, for it was by then apparent that you couldn't really expect to get much more that 13-14mpg out of the car at best, and 11mpg was by no means unusual. The effect on sales of V12 models eventually caused grave concern at Browns Lane, and any thought of the V12 engine taking over entirely from the old XK unit went out of the window.

Compare this with the previous picture. This is the XJ12L, in which the extra 4in is accommodated aft of the centre door pillar, meaning a wider rear door. The XJ6L has exactly the same silhouette.

The long-wheelbase Jaguars were launched at the October 1972 Earls Court Motor Show, where the theme on the Jaguar stand was '50 years – Swallow to Jaguar'. The additional legroom was welcomed by rear-seat passengers.

The longer-wheelbase body was first seen in September 1972, however, when the luxuriously equipped Daimler Double Six Vanden Plas saloon was announced. The 'ordinary' Daimler was offered on this wheelbase a little later, when it was known as the Sovereign LWB.

This in a way was both unfortunate and unfair; unfortunate because the magnificent new V12 engine could certainly lay claim to being the world's best-engineered production power unit, and unfair because, litre-for-litre, it was as fuel efficient as almost any other modern engine. Just its size mitigated against it, particularly on the home and European markets. As a car, the XJ12 was superb, incorporating as it did all the XJ6's refinement and handling qualities, but adding acceleration and top speed that could barely be matched by even the fastest of sports cars, let alone other saloons. And these attributes came in return for an amazingly small outlay in the context of the luxury-car market – £3,725 was the home-market list price for an XJ12, or only slightly more than one-third of the price of the cheapest Rolls-Royce.

Independent road tests soon established that the XJ12 was about the quickest four seater saloon you could buy. *Motor* recorded a 0-60mph time of 7.4 seconds with 100mph coming up in just 19 seconds; and I worked the watches when a similar

car recorded a two-way mean top speed of 135.7mph on the *autostrada* – though our car was the Daimler version, called the 'Double Six' after the memory of the prewar V12-engined Daimler (though this had been a far less satisfactory machine in its time!). Given suitable conditions, the V12 cars could pull well over 6,000rpm in fact, representing a one-way speed of 140mph, or perhaps even a little more.

But perhaps the greatest impression was made not by the car's absolute performance, but rather by the manner in which it was delivered. That superbly smooth, supremely well insulated 12-cylinder engine's presence was under most conditions almost undetectable. *Autocar* probably summed up the matter best when it stated: 'In terms of mechanical quietness, the XJ12 represents the nearest approach yet to a car in which the only sensation of having a propulsive unit under the bonnet is that of speed and acceleration. It is not only the exceptionally low noise level, but the complete absence of any vibration or harshness as well, which makes the car so fantastically docile and effortless.

41

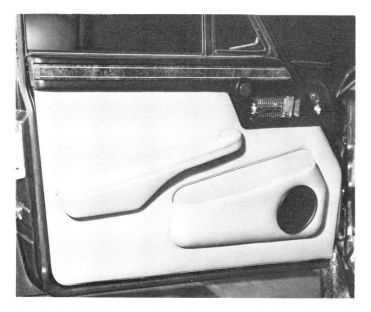

Initially, the VDP Daimler was trimmed and painted at the Vanden Plas works at Kingsbury, but the department was later moved to the Midlands. Jaguar ceased the use of the VDP appellation in 1984.

Extra pressure on the accelerator pedal brings response simply in acceleration without any accompanying power roar or exhaust noise.'

The XJ12's mid-year appearance was not the only new model announcement from Jaguar in 1972. Pursuing Rolls-Royce customers even harder, the Vanden Plas version of the Daimler Double Six arrived in September, this being a normal 12-cylinder car under the skin, but treated to an even more luxurious interior, plus a higher-quality paint finish by Vanden Plas, at Kingsbury, on the outskirts of London. External identification features were a coachline and a vinyl roof. The most expensive Jaguar/Daimler yet, it cost £5,363.

More significantly, though, the Vanden Plas model heralded the most fundamental change yet to the XJ range – a longer wheelbase. The comparative meanness of the rear-seat legroom had been a target for sniping at by the motoring press and some owners for a considerable while, and the XJ was undeniably deficient in this respect compared to some of its rivals. The message got through to Browns Lane and an extra 4 inches was inserted into an otherwise standard XJ bodyshell, increasing the total weight of the car by around 1½cwt and adding about a second to the 0-100mph time of the V12-engined car.

Within a month, at the London Motor Show, similar long-wheelbase versions of the normal Jaguar and Daimler saloons were to be seen on the Jaguar stand, the models designated as XJ6L, XJ12L and Sovereign LWB, though the original-wheelbase cars continued in parallel production; while 583 examples of the XJ6L were completed in RHD form, just one was made in LHD, and only three LHD XJ12Ls, making them about the rarest of all Jaguar saloons! However, the much needed extra inches – which were found not to affect ride or handling to any detectable extent – became standardized for the Series 2 saloons announced a year later, in September 1973 – the date the original XJ family passed into history. After five years during which the type had increased Jaguar's prestige perhaps more than any other model, the XJ was about to undergo its first major facelift.

CHAPTER 4

The Series 2 range

Refinement and a two-door coupe

Like virtually every manufacturer, Jaguar began experimenting with an update directly the original car was safely in production; but thanks to the soundness of design of the first XJs, and their sales success, a revised model was not released until exactly five years to the month after the XJ6's 1968 launch. Indeed, this long span between model changes was and remains a Jaguar tradition and helps to explain further the cars' highly competitive prices over the years – while detail improvements are carried on continuously, costly changes of expensive tooling are avoided. It takes a good car – and one with undated looks – to sustain something like a five-year production run without appearing old-fashioned or dropping behind the opposition.

The Series 2 range came in September 1973, and as the name implied the new cars were improved editions of the old, rather than entirely fresh models, aimed at bringing the XJ up-to-date in relatively small but important ways – because while the cars' ride, handling, performance and refinement were still amongst the best, heating and ventilation, minor controls and general driver convenience were (and perhaps always had been) lagging behind the opposition in varying degrees. 'The Series 2 Jaguars are the outcome of lessons we have learned from the current models – so we haven't changed the concept', was how Jaguar themselves correctly summed-up the changes at the time.

Externally, easily the most obvious change was at the front, where the bumper had been raised to meet bumper-height standardization laws due in the United States the following year. Various front-end styling exercises had been tried which incorporated the new bumper position, but in the end the best and cheapest solution was simply to fit a new, squatter grille and leave the basic headlight and bonnet configuration as before. Sidelights were now under the bumper, and the overriders repositioned each side of the lower air-intake grille. North American cars were given full-width 5mph-impact black 'rubber' bumpers which replaced the rather obtrusive Nordel impact-absorbing overriders which had been fitted as an interim measure. Little was changed at the rear, although the number-plate lamp was repositioned on the bootlid.

However, the car had changed a good deal more than outside appearances suggested, including quite substantial alterations to the bodyshell internals. Specifically, the double-skinned bulkhead had to be sacrificed to provide more room for completely new heating and air-conditioning plants; the heater was now an air-blending unit instead of a water valve-controlled one to allow instant response to the heater controls (which were operated by electric servo motors), and it would maintain a set temperature regardless of the speed or temperature of the incoming air. Throughput was improved as well. The air-conditioner was also uprated (to meet pleas from North American owners) and could now push through 300 instead of 200cu ft/min of cold air.

To counter the lack of a double-skinned bulkhead, Jaguar had gone to a lot of trouble to keep engine and transmission noise down; on the cockpit side, the new bulkhead, together with the footwells and transmission cover, were given layers of bitumised felt and Hardura foam, while new rubber boots and a cowl sealed the clutch/brake pedals and steering column.

Actual air gaps – the most serious cause of noise (and fume) transmission from an engine bay – were eliminated by replacing

As soon as the XJ6 was introduced, Doug Thorpe (then manager of Jaguar's styling department) created this mock-up of a 'Mark 2' version. The full-width grille and resited inner headlights would have meant a new bonnet pressing, so to minimize tooling costs less radical changes were made.

failure-prone grommets with plug sockets and sealed tubes wherever the bulkhead was penetrated. Thus, instead of wires and cables running through the bulkhead, sockets were fixed into it which accepted multi-pin plugs on either side. Heater and refrigeration fluids were conducted in rigid tubes sealed through the bulkhead, flexible tubes running from these to the components. All this made replacement easier as well.

Inside the car, much had changed, although the traditional Jaguar theme of leather and walnut remained. The dash still had a veneered finish, but for the first time on a Jaguar saloon all the instruments (not merely the rev-counter and speedometer) were sited right in front of the driver. The two main instruments were grouped together above the steering column and sandwiched a vertical row of warning lights, though a minus point to some was the rather cheap and 'plasticky' looking moulding which contained them. Larger rectangular air vents replaced the earlier round type at each end of the dash, with another in the centre replacing the minor instruments.

Another big change was the steering wheel; it still had quite a thin rim, but the horn ring was gone and warning was sounded by pressing any part of the big padded centre. When it came to minor controls, the wipers and washers were at last operated by a stalk rather than from amongst a row of 10 switches – which many 'Series 1' drivers had found inconvenient and confusing. But no intermittent-wipe facility was provided yet, and the

blades still did their little dance when 'Park' was selected, though you could lift the stalk for a single wipe. A stalk on the other side of the column worked the indicators, and also the dipswitch, which had previously been foot-operated. The main light switch was now located right alongside the steering column at the bottom of the dash, controlling side, head and foglamps.

The redesign continued elsewhere with the deletion of the parcel shelf on the driver's side, but with an enlarged passenger glove compartment (the lid of which now incorporating a vanity mirror, as on Jaguars of old), front door grab handles and larger armrests, and each rear door now had an ashtray instead of a single one behind the rear heater outlet (which had tended to blow ash everywhere!). More significantly, electrically-operated central locking was offered, although the console-mounted switch was less convenient than the key-operated systems offered by some rivals, and it didn't include the bootlid. Safety was increased by the standardization of laminated windscreen glass throughout the range, and all doors now had 'W' section barriers internally, which were previously only used on some North American cars.

Mechanically, quoted horsepower figures for both the six and 12-cylinder UK cars were down to 170 and 250 respectively, thanks to pollution controls – the XK engine had been given a crossover air intake system which used the exhaust manifold to heat up the mixture prior to induction. (North American cars

The Series 2 saloon, this one being in V12 form. The raised bumper meant repositioning the sidelights underneath, and incorporating a squatter grille.

A USA-specification XJ12L Series 2, showing the full-width 'impact' bumper, repeater lights and round reflectors.

Inside, the dash layout is substantially different on all Series 2 cars. Note the centre vent, the push-switches on the console, a new wheel with padded centre for sounding the horn, a new light switch above the handbrake, and all of the instruments in front of the driver. The overdrive switch is on top of the gear lever.

A smaller rev-counter and speedo were needed to accommodate all the instruments above the steering column. Fibre-optics are used for some of the dash lighting, and note the centre bank of warning lights and the new stalk controls.

had an air pump, too.) A revised exhaust system which dispensed with the relatively troublesome flexible section was fitted; the downpipes now merged into a double-skinned length, which then split into two separate pipes again before entering the silencers. Six-cylinder cars also had a new single-tube oil cooler with the transmission oil on automatic cars being taken into a heat exchanger at the side of the water radiator – the larger engine retained its original arrangements in this respect.

Some useful V12 features were established on the six-cylinder range on the announcement of the Series 2 cars. Besides a fan-cooled battery, the XJ6 was also given the ventilated front discs of the bigger-engined car, and while the original set-up was adequate, the new discs tended to last longer and promote better pad life.

The XJ Coupe
With the launch of the Series 2 Jaguars came news of the most exciting of the XJ range – the two-door coupe. This was

The Series 2 engine bay, with cross-over warm-air intake system, and the fan-cooled battery now used on six-cylinder cars as well.

displayed at most international motor shows from the autumn of 1973, although Jaguar pointed out that it was not yet due for release, and hinted at a 1974 date. In the event, the two-door cars didn't go on sale until April 1975, an early indication of the 'poor sister' role the model was to endure. Difficulties with wind-sealing and a heavy demand for the normal four-door models ensured that Jaguar did not, perhaps, fully concentrate on the coupe's sales potential.

The car was created very much with the North American market in mind – almost every manufacturer there included two-door versions in their range as a matter of course, and these represented a high proportion of sales. But also, it seems that the coupe, with its pillarless side windows, was of particular interest to Sir William himself, and one gets the impression that Jaguar's engineers persevered with the problems of sealing the glass and getting the rear-quarter windows to wind up and down properly because of this. Not that his only previous production car with such styling features was a great success – the SS Airline of 1935 had suffered from body flexing and fumes and was not a favourite of Lyons, but obviously he liked the basic theme – and indeed, as previously related, the Mark X might well have appeared in similar guise.

The new variant was based squarely on the original-wheelbase XJ, sharing its overall dimensions and silhouette. But replacing the four doors were just two, each 4 inches longer

Pillarless coupes had always been a favourite of Sir William Lyons, and early XJ prototypes were very much on the two-door theme.

With the Series 2, Sir William had his wish with the new two-door XJ; there was no centre door pillar, and with both windows wound down it was the next best thing to a soft-top.

The 5.3 version of the coupe; as with the XJ 4.2, front-end styling was identical to the four-door car. The vinyl roof of the coupe was said to be at the insistence of the marketing people – Jaguar would have preferred a painted finish.

than the original front doors to provide better access into the rear via the folding front seat back. As there was no central side pillar, the door glass was sealed against the leading edge of the rear side window, which had a plated frame at this point. Both these windows were electrically-operated, the rear one tilting as it disappeared to avoid the rear wheelarch. When in the closed position, it was kept under tension by a pulley system to increase its rigidity and thus improve the seal with the door glass – a low-pressure area at speed tended to pull the two glasses apart otherwise. This ruse was in fact quite successful and wind noise – at two-figure speeds at least – was not noticeably worse than with a four-door car, particularly as at that time a fair proportion of the latter were leaving Browns Lane with far from perfect seals themselves . . .

Apart from its door/window configuration, the coupe was easily identified externally by its black vinyl roof; this served to emphasize the more sporting nature of the new model (and, incidentally, to reduce time spent 'finishing' the metal roof on the production line – as a few owners who subsequently had the idea of discarding the vinyl and painting the roof instead have

With the phasing-out of the original-wheelbase XJ6 and XJ12 saloons, the coupe alone remained on this wheelbase. Leg room in the rear was therefore adequate rather than generous. This is one of the pre-production cars shown in 1973, which had narrow-pleated leather upholstery.

The interior of an XJ12C, automatic of course, with 'production' wide pleat upholstery. The facia is the normal Series 2 layout. There were Daimler versions, too, including just one (prototype) Vanden Plas.

found to their chagrin!). The 'grained leather' effect also helped disguise the slightly wider rear pillar used on the coupe to improve rigidity and maintain roll-over crush resistance.

Additional stiffness was provided by an extra box-section up inside the door shut face. This, of course, was hidden by the rear quarter trim panel, which also enclosed the inertia reels of the front seat belts. The interior trim conformed to the usual XJ pattern, as did the upholstery, although as mentioned the front

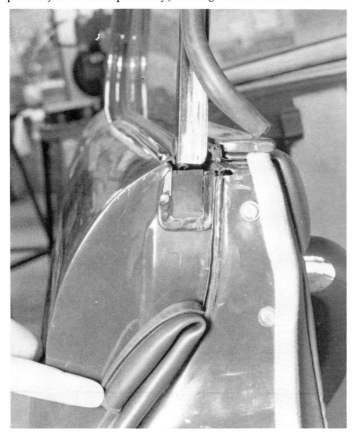

Sealing between side and door windows took some sorting out – a pre-production car is seen here in the experimental trim shop.

seat backs could be released to allow rear passengers to get in and out – which they could then do with reasonable ease. They also enjoyed legroom which was identical to that of the original-wheelbase four-door car. Engine, transmission and running gear were as for the other Series 2 cars, with the choice of six or 12-cylinder engines. Performance was therefore much the same, perhaps slighly better, as the two-door cars weighed about 120lb less than their four-door long-wheelbase counterparts.

The XJ coupe provided something of an alternative to the now very old-fashioned E-type as a sporting Jaguar, offering better handling, a much better ride, more room of course, and (in the case of the V12-engined car) virtually the same straight-line performance as an automatic 2-plus-2 E-type. The only pity was that the same V12 coupe was not offered with a manual gearbox, largely, it seems, because the probable level of demand wouldn't have made it worthwhile for Jaguar to have engineered this option. So it was still only in the E-type that the amazing smoothness, tractability and torque of the magnificent V12 engine at low revs could truly be appreciated – in which it was quite possible to start off in top gear . . .

The coupe was now the only V12-engined example of the original-wheelbase car to remain, as the XJ12 and Daimler Double Six variants of this length were dropped at this stage and so never appeared in Series 2 form. In fact the long wheelbase was adopted as standard at the end of 1974, when the normal-wheelbase XK-engined cars were dropped from the range, too. There were Daimler versions of the coupe, but these varied only in the usual items of minor trim and the 'crinkle cut' radiator shell; they were termed the Daimler Sovereign Two-Door and the Daimler Double Six Two-Door.

Simultaneously with the announcement of the coupe models came the news that Jaguar were adopting fuel injection for the V12 engine, though for the first few months its application was confined to the two-door models – perhaps with a view to getting the system and its manufacture 'run in' prior to going into full production. Better emission control and economy were the main reasons for getting rid of carburettors – the oil crisis of 1973 had drastically affected the sales of big-engined cars the world over, and the XJ12 was no exception, while for 1975 much cleaner engines were required in the United States.

As recounted earlier, Jaguar had wanted to use fuel injection at the onset of V12 engine production, but Brico had cancelled its plans to make a suitable system at that time. However, the company had continued to work with Lucas, who were also developing a fuel injection system, this one having been originated by Bendix and then put into production by Bosch after further work as the Jetronic system of 1967. As it stood it could not be used on engines with more than eight cylinders, so Lucas and Jaguar engineers redeveloped it for 12-cylinder use.

The heart of the system was a computor control unit which took into account water and air temperatures, manifold pressure and engine speed, enabling a very precise amount of fuel to be delivered to each cylinder, exactly meeting the demands of the engine. A separate injector on each inlet manifold provided additional fuel during a cold start until automatically cut out by a water thermostat. Power was now stated to be 285bhp at 5,750rpm (250rpm lower than before), a 32bhp improvement.

In practice, the system worked extremely well, though perhaps the most immediately noticeable benefits were ease of starting, untemperamental running when cold and even greater smoothness and crispness when warm rather than just the (welcome) improvement in fuel economy. Certainly that was there, however, assisted by a higher axle ratio (3.07 instead of 3.31), and it was now possible to obtain more than 15mpg if restraint was exercised; but in average use the injected V12s still hovered around the 13-14mpg mark, and could guzzle petrol at the rate of 11 or 12mpg if driven hard. A battle in the fight against fuel consumption had been won, but total victory was still some way off.

The percentage improvement was considerable – *Autocar* tested an XJ5.3C in November 1975 and found that it was 21% more economical than the carburettor-equipped XJ12 saloon they'd tried earlier, at 13.8mpg against 11.4mpg. This served to increase the car's range, too, despite a small reduction in tank capacity, the 20 gallons now lasting 270 miles or so as opposed to a little over 200. A worthwhile factor to the high-mileage business user.

This same coupe turned out to be a little slower than *Autocar*'s original XJ12 saloon, possibly due to the higher axle ratio; at 13.1 seconds, the coupe took 1.1 seconds more to reach 80mph from a standstill, and 2.3 seconds longer (at 10.3 seconds) to accelerate from 40 to 80mph. Still highly impressive, though,

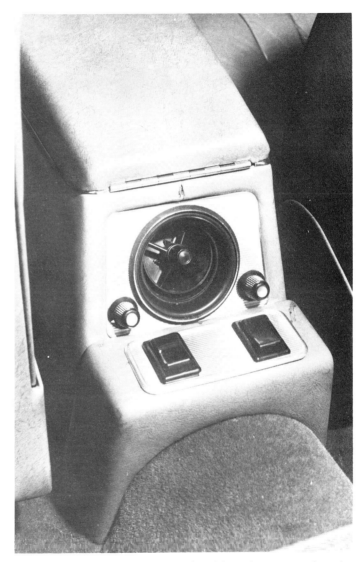

On the Series 2, the ashtray was transferred from the rear console to the doors and replaced by the electric window switches.

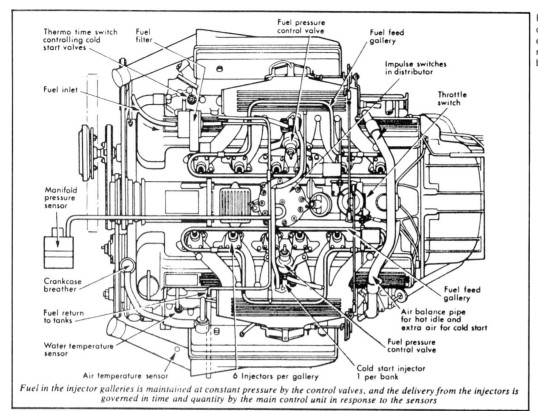

Thermo time switch controlling cold start valves

Fuel filter

Fuel pressure control valve

Fuel feed gallery

Impulse switches in distributor

Throttle switch

Fuel inlet

Manifold pressure sensor

Crankcase breather

Fuel return to tanks

Water temperature sensor

Air temperature sensor

6 Injectors per gallery

Cold start injector 1 per bank

Fuel feed gallery

Air balance pipe for hot idle and extra air for cold start

Fuel pressure control valve

Fuel in the injector galleries is maintained at constant pressure by the control valves, and the delivery from the injectors is governed in time and quantity by the main control unit in response to the sensors

Fuel injection, for better economy and a cleaner exhaust, arrived at last for the V12 engine in 1975, the year when emission regulations in the United States really began to bite.

and the journal found that the road behaviour continued to live up to the speeds obtainable: '. . . the ride of the XJ series has been refined to the very highest standards and one is very hard put indeed to find cars to rival it . . . handling on wet roads is a revelation bordering on the magical.' Top speed was a resounding 147mph!

The XJ 3.4

But the greatest potential for producing an economical Jaguar still lay with the trusty old straight-six engine, and April 1975 also saw Jaguar reintroduce a 3.4-litre version of the XK power unit. The original 3.4-litre block was no longer in production, so the new variant was based on the current 4.2 block with its staggered bores, though the familiar bore and stroke of 83 × 106mm gave the equally familiar capacity of 3,442cc. The existing 4.2-type cylinder head was used, complete with two HS8 carburettors, and the quoted output of 161bhp at 5,000rpm reflected the increased honesty of manufacturers' horsepower figures by this time (the 2.8-litre had originally been rated at 180bhp!).

This unit was installed in the four-door XJ shell only, though it was offered in both Jaguar and Daimler form; either a four-

The injection V12 engine in 1975 'emission' form, complete with air injection pump. This is a left-hand-drive car, of course.

speed synchromesh gearbox with overdrive or a Borg-Warner Model 65 automatic transmission could be specified, both arriving with a 3.54 rear axle ratio instead of the 4.2's 3.31. In order to make the price even more competitive, the 3.4 didn't come with the electric windows and central door locking that had been standardized on the 4.2, and polyester cloth seats replaced leather (cloth became an option on the larger-engined models, too). At £4,794 on the home market, the new 3.4 was a useful £342 less than the cheapest 4.2, which just about brought it in range of someone who otherwise might have settled for a Rover or a Ford with all the options. The car wasn't seen in North America, however, which although now petrol-conscious, was thought still to prefer the extra performance of the 4.2 or 5.3 cars – and certainly an XJ 3.4 laden with full Californian emission control equipment would have been a little sluggish.

The 3.4 was well received by the motoring press in the UK.

Autocar pronounced that the 'new' engine was 'remarkably smooth and refined, certainly more so than its bigger brother', which showed that the revised block with its additional external ribbing and the modified crank with redesigned webs were doing their job – although it's generally acknowledged that the 3.4 edition of the XK engine, of whatever age, was always the smoothest. It also provided a very adequate performance, 0-60mph arriving in 10.9 seconds, 2.2 seconds down on the 4.2-litre the magazine had tried in 1971. Top speed was 115mph in overdrive top, as opposed to just under 125mph for the larger-engined car.

Where the reduced capacity made itself felt was, predictably, when the engine was asked to pull from low revs. Said *Autocar*, 'for those used to the 4.2 litre, there is no doubt the engine lacks punch . . . if one is to make consistently rapid progress, much more use must be made of the gears'. Thus the 30-50mph top-gear increment of 9.5 seconds was beaten by such as the new

The XJ 3.4 was an important factor in reducing the cost of becoming the owner of a new Jaguar; it also appealed to those who liked the comfort of the Jaguar but could do without the thirst – and extra performance – of the larger-engined versions. To keep the price down, cloth upholstery was standard (though leather could be ordered as an option). Electric windows were also an extra.

Rover 3500 SD1 at 7.9 seconds and the 3-litre Ford Granada, which recorded 8.3 seconds. But the 4.2 manual/overdrive XJ6 returned an exemplary 6.5 seconds so it was a case of paying your money and taking your choice – and if you took economy as a priority, the 3.4 was very frugal for a Jaguar, *Motor* recording 20mpg overall and reckoning that over 23mpg was possible; *Autocar* didn't match this, however, their overall consumption working out at 16.7mpg.

A brief comparison with the previous 'economy' XJ, the 2.8-litre, might be interesting here, and with the original 3.4-litre Mark 1 saloon of the late 1950s. Thanks mainly to its low-ratio 4.55 axle, the 2.8 could equal the XJ 3.4's 0-60mph time of around 11 seconds, and was actually faster to 100mph and (at 117mph) in top speed; it also offered about the same fuel consumption, but of course its reliability record was not good. It did, incidentally, appear briefly in Series 2 form, but only in a few European countries, and it had been discontinued by the time the XJ 3.4 arrived. The 3.4-litre of 1957 could run the pants off both in a straight line, however, reaching 60mph in 9.1 seconds, bridging the 30-50mph gap in 6.7 seconds, and being

capable of 120mph flat out. But then it weighed some 3cwt less than the 33cwt XJ 3.4 and had a lower (3.77 instead of 3.54) axle ratio. Petrol consumption was about 16mpg, incidentally. In all other respects, the old 3.4 was totally outclassed, needless to say – but the figures do underline that it, too, in its time, was pretty astonishing for a luxury four-seater.

Detail improvement of the XJ range continued during the 1970s, though a more substantial change was the adoption of the General Motors Turbo Hydramatic gearbox on all the 5.3-litre cars in April 1977. The GM 400 box superseded the Borg-Warner Model 12 unit, and while it shared the same quadrant layout ('PRND21', though there was increased selector lever travel between 'P' and 'R'), it was much more responsive to throttle input, and gave the driver the opportunity of selecting first gear manually – formerly this could only be obtained by kick-down from 'D'. Second gear could also be held by the driver to the 6,500rpm maximum.

The changes were smoother, if anything, and about the only criticism that could be made concerned the illogical nature of the selector, which still had the unnecessary detent between 'D' and '2', and the lack of same between 'D' and 'N' (it was all too easy, when returning the lever from '2' to 'D', to overshoot into 'N'). Jaguar, incidentally, carried out a fairly extensive re-engineering programme on the transmission; as with previous American designs, in standard form the change points were more suited to low-revving V8 engines and, according to Jaguar's engineering department, the unit could not reliably accept the power, torque and revs of the 5.3 V12 without considerable modification.

The new box was assessed along with all the other aspects of the now fuel-injected V12 saloon by *Autocar* in September 1978. Noting that the XJ12 now cost 47% of the price of a Rolls-Royce Silver Shadow · (in 1978 it was 38%), they nevertheless commented that the car, 'in its combination of performance, road behaviour and refinement . . . is still unsurpassed'. The fuel injection ensured that the engine started from cold with no temperament whatever, and the virtually undetectable gearchanges helped the car to 'glide through town in eerie quietness – a quietness of two sorts, compounded of the excellent mechanical refinement of engine and running gear and of the superlative insulation against exterior noise provided by the body when all the windows are up'.

Performance was only marginally down on the 220lb lighter normal-wheelbase XJ12 tested in 1973, despite the higher gearing of the newer car, with 100mph coming up in 19 seconds instead of 18.8. Top speed was a remarkable 147mph and, as *Autocar* pointed out, 'even if the XJ5.3 driver never approaches such heights, he knows that such a capability is one of the main reasons why the car is so magnificent in performance *and* refinement *and* safety at lesser speeds'. At 13.2mph overall, the V12 saloon was hardly economical, but the magazine found that with restraint, 15-16mpg was possible – and that a simple calculation, taking into account the XJ's 37cwt, showed that the car was just as fuel efficient as a Porsche 911 or Lotus Elite.

Under the heading of 'Road Behaviour', the XJ was described as 'almost impeccable' with very little roll, excellent grip in wet or dry, and 'perhaps the best ride compromise achieved by *any* manufacturer'. The steering needed a 'delicate touch – you learn to drive the car with the fingertips rather than the hands', and escaped too much criticism for being over-light, a fairly frequent complaint by road-testers over the years (Jaguar never

The Daimler was produced in smaller-engined form as well and called the Sovereign 3.4.

really accepted this point, saying, quite rightly, that their customers never complained!).

Irritations included the 'extraordinary out-of-date Lucas two-speed wipers', the lack of an interrupted wipe facility, and areas of the screen left unswept; it was also felt that seat height should be variable, and other niggles concerned the over-complicated nature of the central door locking (you couldn't just put the key in the driver's lock and turn it, as with Mercedes, and it still didn't include the boot in its circuitry), the 'crude-feeling gearbox selector' with the 'almost dangerous lack of anything to stop you going into Neutral from 'D' ', the shallowness of the boot, and the occasional propensity of one corner of the bonnet not to stay shut.

Of course, the XJ saloons were road-tested in North America, too, and *Road & Track* magazine tested an XJ12 with the new gearbox in 1977. Generally it agreed with its British counterparts, though as on previous occasions it qualified its

Fuel-injection was standardized on the V12 saloon during 1975, at which time a vinyl roof was adopted; this car is also fitted with the optional new GKN alloy wheels.

The same year saw the introduction of a Vanden Plas version of the Sovereign 4.2 which, like the VDP Double-Six, has 'individual' rear seats and a very full specification.

North Americans loved their XJs, but during the latter half of the 1970s they were sometimes in despair over their build quality. Otherwise enthusiastic road-test reports of the period always seemed to be qualified by doubts about the cars' reliability. Note the 5mph impact bumpers and repeater-lights.

praise by saying that Jaguar never seemed to hurry through new models or changes 'no matter how badly they're needed. This has always been one of the frustrating aspects of owning a Jaguar: knowing how great the car could be if some of the niggling problems and details had been worked out more carefully.' But with the latest version of the 12-cylinder car the journal could find comparatively little to fault (that gear selector was one item!) and *R&T* ended its brief test report by relating that they were 'glad to see one of the world's best cars get better'.

Performance of this saloon was down on its European opposite number, though, as the engine was hampered by detoxing equipment and an 8:1 compression ratio to enable it to run on 91-octane unleaded fuel. A speed of 100mph thus took 23.5 seconds to reach and top speed was 128mph (at 5,700rpm). 'Normal driving' gave a reasonably respectable 13mpg, which is better than it seems because a US gallon is only just over 83% of an Imperial gallon.

But to some extent the opposition was catching up with the Series 2 XJ, and when *Road & Track* matched the same XJ12 against a Mercedes-Benz 450 SEL and one of the new 733i

BMWs, it lost out to both. So far as ride and handling were concerned, the Jaguar was the softest of the three and tended to float and occasionally 'bottom' over bumps, with the 'overly light' steering combining with this to inhibit the full use of the car's excellent handling. Nor did the brakes perform as efficiently as the German cars'. 'If the BMW is delightful and the Mercedes serious', asked *R&T*, 'what is the Jaguar? Elegant of course, but is that what it needs to be the best of the three?' So the BMW was unanimously voted the best by the journal's test staff – they still loved the Jaguar, but 'she is ageing . . .' However, it is clear that *R&T* placed more emphasis on sporting behaviour than on silence, comfort and sheer luxury on this occasion.

One important aspect which is very much part of the XJ's story is the reliability factor, and this affected sales as much as or, possibly, more than any other. *Road & Track* investigated this topic in June 1978, when they conducted an Owner's Survey. As for why people bought an XJ in the first place, an overwhelming 94% of owners listed styling as an influence, 85% were impressed by the car's handling, 79% listed comfort and

78% ride quality. Surprisingly, a large proportion (57%, a record) said they drove the Jaguar moderately, only 7% ticking 'very hard', while 57% used the car for long trips and holidays, a low proportion in view of the XJ's suitability for such work.

Owners were then asked to list problems, which were then subdivided by the magazine into reliability areas, that is, where the problem made the car impossible or unsafe to drive. On this basis the XJ range ranked in third place on *R&T*'s list of least reliable cars, with 21 problem areas for the 12-cylinder car and 19 for the 'six'. Only the Rover 2000TC of 1970 and the Lotus Elan of 1971 were worse, with 24 and 22 problem areas, respectively.

Broken down (an apt phrase . . .) these areas could be defined as including eight reliability areas, with the cooling system topping the list – it was mentioned by one-third of XJ6 owners and a half of XJ12 owners. Overheating was the main trouble, in a few instances leading to head and valve problems 'and even a couple of cracked engine blocks'. Next came electrical items, alternators or voltage regulators needing attention on a third of the XJ6s and 20% of the XJ12s. Other electrical ailments (those which didn't actually stop the car running properly) were encountered by 22% of the XJ6 owners and 14% of the XJ12 drivers. Instrument troubles were reported on 24% of the XJ6s and 30% of the XJ12s, while oil leaks and ignition failures afflicted 30% and 25% of the two models, respectively. Parts were rated as 'expensive' by 83% of owners, and as for the official dealers who were supposed to fix all these faults, only one other make (Opel, in 1973) got a worse rating than the 34% of Jaguar owners who marked theirs down as 'poor'. Only 60% of owners said they'd buy another Jaguar. 'I'd love to buy another, but commonsense says no' appears to have been a typical comment.

It is hardly any wonder, therefore, that Jaguar made no real sales progress in North America during the last half of the 1970s. Quality control at Browns Lane was probably worse than it had ever been in the company's history, and while few of the faults could be put down to poor design of fundamental components, a lack of concern by outside suppliers, coupled with Jaguar's apparent inability to enforce standards with these and their own workforce, led to fairly widespread loss of confidence in the product by dealers and customers alike.' Changes at the helm hadn't helped, either.

Sir William Lyons had retired in March 1972 as Chairman and Chief Executive, after close on 50 years of SS and Jaguar, completing a career of almost unmatched achievement and distinction in the motor industry. He was succeeded by F.W.R. 'Lofty' England, who had become Deputy Chairman in 1967 – but as he too was nearing retirement age, BL brought in Geoffrey Robinson as Managing Director in September 1973. Robinson, who had previously revamped BL's Innocenti plant in Italy, certainly realized that Jaguar was special and that its engineering had to be maintained independently of BL (which

The police continued to employ the XJ6, in Series 2 form, especially for motorway work. This is the Staffordshire police motorway fleet in 1974.

An XJ special. As the factory had long since given up producing open Jaguars, the specialist coachbuilding trade stepped in. The two-door was the most popular candidate for turning into a convertible – this is the Avon-Stevens version.

at that time was hell-bent on carrying out the Ryder Plan, which demanded a merging of makes into a corporate conglomerate), but he placed more emphasis on increased production than on improving the quality of what was already being made.

The 4.2 Series 2 saloon, meanwhile, had continued to be the backbone of Jaguar's production, the 12-cylinder and 'small six' cars making up a relatively small proportion of overall sales. *Autocar* tried an automatic version during 1977 and found that while it had put on weight (by a hundredweight over the 33.5cwt Daimler Sovereign they'd tried in 1974), and while the quoted 180bhp remained the same, efficiency had been improved so that 15mpg overall was obtained instead of the 1974 figure of 14.3mpg. Acceleration was only slightly down, the newer car taking 3.3 seconds longer to reach 100mph.

Like *Road & Track*, the British journal felt that the car's springing and damping were 'a shade on the soft side . . . though by no means subject to the "heave" of the typical American car'. The rather inept wiper controls and gearbox selector again came in for criticism, but despite the XJ6 no longer representing such 'crushing value for money' as it did in 1968, 'there is a sense of astonishment that so old a design should remain not merely competitive, but should still set the highest standards in the highest of classes – not across the board, naturally, but in many

important areas'.

Lack of investment had also contributed to Jaguar's reliability problems during the XJ's production career up to this time, as profits had been absorbed by British Leyland to offset its own huge losses instead of being used to engineer-out problem areas and introduce new models and improvements. Jaguar, of course, had joined forces with Leyland when British Motor Holdings, the company formed by the merger of Jaguar and BMC in 1967, combined with Leyland in May 1968 to form the British Leyland Motor Corporation. Theoretically, Jaguar's autonomy was established by Lyons before he left, but in the years that followed it was a very close run thing, when only the determination of men like England, Robinson (for a short while), Plant Director Peter Craig and Bob Knight prevented the Jaguar identity from sinking without trace in the rush to submerge individual marques by BLMC management.

So far as money was concerned, Lofty England records that the situation improved in 1973, when Jaguar were allowed more funds; much of this went on Geoffrey Robinson's campaign to increase output (though he never quite matched the record year of 1971, when 32,589 Jaguars and Daimlers left the works) and perhaps not enough on strengthening the company's engineering resources at a time when giant competitors like

Mercedes and BMW were ploughing huge sums into the ever more expensive field of research and development.

During 1975, Robinson resigned after being thwarted by the continued implementation of the Ryder Plan – which denied him the sums he required to meet his rather optimistic goal of doubling production to 60,000 cars a year, and denied the company even a management board of its own. Bob Knight became Managing Director in 1978, after fighting long and hard for the company's independence, the year in which Michael Edwardes began his attempt to salvage BL; retaining most of the old marque names became a key part of his policy, but for a further two unhappy years Jaguar was lumped in with Rover and Triumph to operate as 'JRT', during which period morale at Browns Lane sunk to a very low ebb.

It was the Series 2 Jaguars – along with the XJ-S which came along in 1975 – that had to live through all this turmoil, and it is no wonder that quality sometimes suffered, with neither management (what was left of it) nor the workforce knowing what was coming next. The car itself was beautifully engineered and significantly better than the Series 1 it had replaced in almost every way, but these internal problems, plus the worldwide decrease in popularity of thirsty motor cars, effectively stunted its growth. Meanwhile, though, Jaguar's engineering division had been persevering with the work of improving the car still further, particularly in the region of efficiency.

This was because, particularly in the United States, emission control equipment involving air injection and exhaust gas recirculation, had seriously reduced the car's performance and economy. 'In common with most manufacturers selling cars in North America, we were unhappy with the serious losses in efficiency which were inevitable with the earlier emission control techniques, which took a lot of sparkle out of the performance and made the car thirstier', said Harry Mundy, the ex-Coventry Climax man who had become Director of Power Unit and Transmission Engineering.

One course of action would have been to reduce the XJ's weight, but this couldn't be achieved without going to a new bodyshell, and anyway, as the car gained more and more equipment as standard, the *avoir dupois* would continue to spiral upwards. So Jaguar's engineers did about the only thing they could do – improve the engine of the most popular model, the 4.2, so that it produced more horsepower more efficiently. This was not simply a sales booster, though, as the company was already having to pay what was nicknamed the 'gas guzzler' tax on its exports to the United States – here, financial penalties were exacted on any company whose cars' fuel consumption (taken as the average of the entire range imported) fell below a set figure. An extra few mpg from the most widely imported Jaguar would therefore help a lot in reducing the average consumption of the range.

The answer was to modify the 4.2 to run on fuel injection instead of carburettors. This was not the first time the XK engine had been so equipped as the later D-types and the lightweight E-types had used a Lucas mechanical system, but this time Bosch/Lucas L-Jetronic equipment was employed, together with larger inlet valves (the new arrangement is fully described in the next chapter). The installation was a great success, and in May 1978 North American XJ 4.2s featured the system as standard. Horsepower went up from 162 to 176bhp (still at 4,750rpm) and fuel consumption went down from around 15mpg to 17mpg-plus, despite a three-way catalytic converter.

Fuel injection gave the Series 2 a new lease of life in America, where the improvements were received almost rapturously; 'the injected six is so good it nearly makes us forget the lovely sound and strength of the V12' said *Road & Track* of its test car, reporting a 'normal driving' petrol consumption of 17½ miles per US gallon. *Car and Driver* waxed even more lyrical; sub-heading his test report with the phrase 'so good it's probably immoral', David E. Davis went on to say that if a Mercedes is like a beautifully made tool and a BMW like a very good camera or shotgun, 'a Jaguar is like the highest quality, custom-made ladies' underwear. It is so slippery and tactile that the Baptists probably have a law against it.'

The steering was felt to be a little light and the suspension a little soft for really fast cornering, and of course the statutory denigration of Joseph Lucas ('the people who invented darkness') was included, but generally it was thought that the XJ6 had stood the test of time well. 'And maybe, just maybe, something will happen to give it several more years of life.'

That something was just around the corner.

CHAPTER 5

The Series 3 range

A new look and a new image

The second and most extensive revision of the XJ saloons once again coincided with the end of a five-year span, when on March 29, 1979 the Series 2 became obsolete and the Series 3 made its entrance. Visually, the car had undergone quite significant changes, and its specification had been improved, altered or added to in many different ways. Little had been done to upset the traditionalists, but much had been accomplished in making the XJ a car for the 1980s – a not-inconsiderable feat with a design now basically 10 years old!

While the bodyshell below the waistline remained substantially unaltered, the top portion was given what could be termed a 'crew-cut', with metal area reduced, glass area increased, and the car's profile generally sharpened up. This was achieved by decreasing the slope of the roof towards the rear, giving a more angular appearance from the side, flattening the back window a little, extending the depth of the glass along the sides and increasing the rake of the front screen pillars by 3 inches. The tumble-home of the side windows from the waistline was also increased by making the actual roof panel narrower, while the deletion of the front quarter-light posts also contributed to a cleaner look.

These changes were accompanied by new flush-fitting exterior door handles of the 'lift and pull' type, new stainless-steel wheel trims, and new bumpers covered by black injection mouldings with brightwork cappings – these, on home-market cars, looked very similar to the '5mph-impact' bumpers on North American cars, but were actually without the impact-absorbing beams behind. The front bumpers now incorporated the indicator lights, and as the sidelights were contained in the headlamps, there were now no secondary lamp housings in the wings.

Also at the front was a new radiator grille, a simpler and altogether more pleasing design than before, having vertical slats reminiscent of the Series 1 XJ12's. The rear aspect of the car was mostly altered in appearance by the new light cluster which now incorporated reversing lights, and the redesigned number-plate lamp housing and boot handle – wider and flatter, the new housing ran the width of the number-plate. Rear badging was now in matt black, with the maker's name (either Jaguar or Daimler) on the left and the model designation on the right.

While some enthusiasts for the early Series 1 cars may not entirely agree, these exterior changes were probably for the better, making the Series 3 XJ an even more handsome car than its predecessors – which is something that couldn't always be said of previous Jaguar model updates! Interestingly, Giorgetto Giugiaro, perhaps the most outstanding car stylist of our time, recently nominated the XJ6 as one of the most beautiful cars in the world – and specifically chose the Series 3 expression of the XJ theme. The changes were carried out in conjunction with the advice of Pininfarina, certainly the first time (to my knowledge) that an outside styling consultant had been used by Jaguar. Of course, Sir William's opinion was sought, too – it was still highly valued, and indeed was to remain so in the years ahead.

But the updating procedure was taken to much greater lengths inside the car and in its detail specification – leaving aside for a moment the car's mechanical aspects, Jaguar really had listened to the marketplace this time, and a host of sensible

Cleaner, sleeker lines, black bumpers and recessed door handles all help to distinguish the Series 3 model. Early 'photographic' cars like this were fitted with dummy number-plates by the factory, reflecting famous Jaguars of the past – OKV 3 was a 1954 works D-type, the first of its kind to win a race. Hardly anyone noticed, though!

improvements and much-needed additions were to be found in the Series 3. These brought the car far more in line with its contemporaries in the luxury-car field, as indeed needed to happen if the basic design was to be kept totally competitive for yet another five-year period.

The list was impressive: standard fittings now included new front seats with adjustable lumber support, interior light delay, stereo radio/cassette with electric aerial delay, 'timed' heated rear window (it switched itself off after 15 minutes to prevent unnecessary current drain), quartz-halogen headlights and (loud cheers all round) a two-speed windscreen wiper system, which at last was self-parking *and* included a 6-second delayed action facility – this without losing the flick-wipe mode, the more credit to Jaguar.

Important new extras were offered, too – an electrically operated steel sunroof, electrically operated door mirrors, cruise control, headlamp wash/wipe and electric driver's seat height adjustment whereby the seat cushion could be raised or lowered through an arc of almost 2 inches, pivotted at the front (this was a standard fitting to both front seats of the Daimler Vanden Plas, as were the headlamp wash/wipe and electric mirrors; USA-specification Series 3s had the cruise control as

standard). These were all in addition to the previous extras such as air conditioning, inertia-reel rear seat belts, more expensive tape player/radio and light-alloy wheels of the XJ-S pattern.

The new owner of a Series 3 Jaguar was also presented with a revised interior; immediately obvious was the increased glass area and rear headroom, all of which made the car feel lighter and more airy to sit in, while the seats, with their new range of adjustments, also incorporated an additional 1½ inches in the backrest for extra support. The seat backs were also given better headrests, and there were map pockets for the use of rear passengers – who were also provided with more footroom by virtue of the front seat-belt inertia reels being hidden away in the centre door pillars. A new headlining incorporating recessed sun-visors was installed, and a larger rear-view mirror fitted. Underfoot was a new deep-pile carpet, and vacuum-formed rubber and plastic foam mouldings behind the door panels and on the bulkhead and prop-shaft tunnel contributed further to noise suppression.

The dashboard and facia layout was basically as on the Series 2, though switches and minor instruments were now annotated with international symbols rather than numbers, and the steering column control stalks were transposed, again with an

Electronic fuel-injection gave the sturdy old XK engine a new lease of life – power was now around a genuine 200bhp for European cars; North American cars had dispensed with carburettors the previous year.

Alone of the range – excepting the Mark X-based, 4.2-engined Daimler limousine – the 3.4 saloon remained on carburettors. With its sales restricted to outside the USA, the cheapness of the two SU carburettors has been more important than a slightly cleaner exhaust.

Seats on the Series 3 are plusher, with wider pleats and revised shapes for both cushion and squab. Deletion of quarter-lights contributes to the wider glass area. The leather-rimmed steering wheel with revised centre is another Series 3 feature.

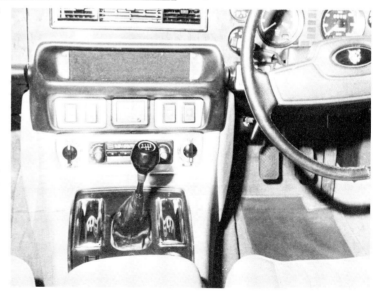

The new five-speed gearbox has been of great appeal to the enthusiast-driver – top is a dog-leg movement to the right and up. The manual-gearbox car is some 1½ seconds quicker to 60mph and around 10% more economical than the automatic version.

eye on world markets. Additions were made to the bank of warning lights between rev-counter and speedometer (the latter now with both mph and kph lettering) to monitor low coolant level and operation of rear foglamps. In addition, if a side or brake light failed, a warning light on the speedometer face would illuminate. The central locking device now included the bootlid in its circuitry, while the driver was provided with three keys – one for ignition, a master key which fitted everything, and a 'service key' which unlocked only the doors and the fuel filler caps.

Complementing all the additional equipment and the car's new shape was a range of new paint colours, eight in all, plus black and Sebring Red to special order; many of these were metallic, such as Cobalt Blue, Platinum and Chestnut, and they were all applied at a specially built and very expensive plant at Castle Bromwich, where the XJ bodies were being made. The new arrangement was not without its problems, however, and there were difficulties both in applying the new thermoplastic acrylic paint and in keeping it in good condition on the subsequent journey to Browns Lane, where the painted shell

Series 3 rear passengers enjoy greater headroom, and more footroom, thanks to front seat-belt reels being hidden away. Map pockets appeared in the front seat backs, but these rear seat-belts were still an optional extra.

The Series 3 boot. Tools are contained in an attache case and the warning triangle and jack are on the left.

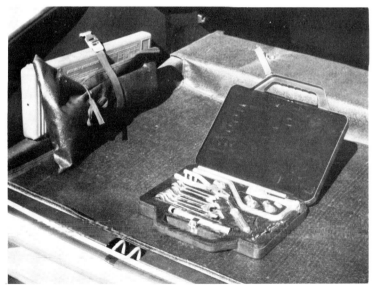

was fitted-up. For the first few months of Series 3 production, it seemed as though you could get any colour you liked so long as it was white . . . Eventually, through the use of special trucks and sheer experience, the main problems were solved and basically the same system is in use today.

On the mechanical side, the big news with the coming of the Series 3 centred around the 4.2-litre car, where fuel injection now replaced carburettors. As previously related, North American XJ6s had been so equipped for almost a year, and it was logical that the remainder of the market should also benefit from the increased efficiency the system brought.

The most obvious result bestowed by the Lucas/Bosch L-Jetronic injection was the 30bhp power increase – perhaps the biggest genuine percentage power boost the XK engine ever received in its production life. All of this was available for direct use, too, as of course the European market cars were not required to carry the three-way catalytic converter needed for the North American market. The operation of the system was similar to the V12 engine's, an electronic control unit receiving data from sensors in the engine, computing the fuel

A 'Federal' Series 3 saloon, with 5mph-impact bumpers, similar to the car tried by *Road & Track*, who recorded a top speed of 117mph despite 'only' 176bhp from the 'emission' six-cylinder engine.

Inside, the USA-specification XJ6 looks very similar to the British version – except that an increasing amount of equipment is included in the standard specification.

requirements and transmitting the correct impulses to the injector solenoids. Fuel was supplied by a single high-pressure pump at a constant 36psi, with unused petrol being returned to the tanks via a separate line. A separate cold-start circuit, with its own injector, delivered extra fuel until shut off by a thermo-time switch.

The accuracy of the fuel charge ensured much better efficiency, and fuel consumption was also helped by an overrun fuel cut-off; this operated when the throttle was closed, providing engine revs were kept above 1,200rpm – at this point fuel was allowed to flow again. The compression ratio on home-market cars went up from 7.8 to 8.7:1 due to the use of the old '9:1' pistons, and larger inlet valves also contributed to the better performance; their diameter of 1$\frac{7}{8}$in was immediately familiar to D-type Jaguar owners or anyone who modified XK engines for racing as this size of inlet valve had been commonly used for competition Jaguars since 1954.

So the 4.2-litre XK engine now churned out some 200bhp at

The V12-engined Series 3 saloon carried similar updates to the 4.2 and 3.4-litre version on its announcement in 1979.

the flywheel to become the most powerful six-cylinder unit Jaguar had put into series production (earlier quoted outputs of 265bhp for the 3.8 and 4.2 engines were exaggerations issued to match equally optimistic figures claimed by American manufacturers during the horsepower race of the 1960s), and it could be mated to a five-speed gearbox, the so-called Rover SD1 '77mm' (the dimension of the shafts) box, which had been announced for XJ saloons a few months previously, at the 1978 London Motor Show (though seemingly not introduced then).

This gearbox stemmed from a Harry Mundy design which, with its 88mm mainshaft, was intended for use with the V12 engine; this latter five-speed box did not, alas, get to the production stage as customer demand for a manual transmission was at a low ebb. Indeed, Jaguar's adoption of the 77mm box meant the demise of the old four-speeder, which alone had been capable of handling the 5.3 engine's power and torque, so the manual option on the XJ-S was discontinued. It was simply not commercially viable to build the 88mm box for the envisaged

small demand and any hope that an XJ12 saloon would ever be offered with manual transmission also vanished.

Instead, work continued on a two-speed axle, which was designed to take the place of the Laycock overdrive unit, and be used on manual and automatic XJ6s as well as on cars powered by the V12 engine, which was too powerful for the overdrive to cope with. The two-speed axle would have been a useful aid to economy, but in the end it was not proceeded with, probably because of cost and the increased efficiency of the power units themselves.

The new gearbox was a no-cost option on the 3.4 and 4.2-litre cars, except on the Daimler Vanden Plas 4.2, which came only with automatic transmission. The addition of a fifth gear allowed closer ratios (which tended to help acceleration), but the new fifth did not quite match the old overdrive ratio for long legged cruising – for instance, with a 3.54 final drive (as used for the 3.4 car) it gave 25.8mph per 1,000rpm, compared with the 27.5mph provided by the Laycock device. While the few drivers

The Daimler Sovereign continued in either 4.2 or 3.4-litre guise on the announcement of the Series 3 range, though the Daimler name had only a few more years to run before being discontinued outside Great Britain.

who specified the manual gearbox may have missed the finger-tip change facility of the old overdrive unit, the five-speed box quickly gained acceptance and, overall, it was more practical and reliable than the previous arrangement; it was also 30lb lighter than the old gearbox/overdrive assembly, and weight-saving was becoming an increasing priority.

As for the V12-engined car, only detail changes occurred to the mechanical specification and the power output of the already-injected engine remained at 285bhp at 5,750rpm. Elsewhere it shared all the new Series 3 features, including a price rise – the Series 3 cars were some 11% dearer than their predecessors, indicative of BL's pricing policy, which had pushed Jaguar prices up by something like £1,000 per year since 1973, more than making up for inflation. Significantly, the £20,000 barrier was broken for the first time, as the top-of-the range Daimler Double-Six Vanden Plas came out at £20,277.27.

The new model was well received, even if the troublesome Castle Bromwich paintshop prevented a good supply of cars reaching customers immediately. Most observers rated the styling improvements a success, the revised controls and

equipment were welcomed, and everyone agreed that fuel injection had given the old long-stroke 'six' a new lease of life, if not the whole car. *Autocar*, in its December 1979 road test of an automatic 4.2, labelled the performance 'dramatically better', this being particularly noticeable in higher speed ranges; while the 0-60mph time of 10.0 seconds was only just over half a second better than the Series 2 could manage, 100mph was attained in 29.4 seconds as opposed to 34.1 seconds, while at 38.5 seconds, the 110mph figure was 'a remarkable 13.3 seconds quicker than before'. Top speed on the 3.07 axle ratio was 127mph mean, compared to the 117mph of the 4.2-litre Series 2.

Equally importantly, fuel economy had also benefited, *Autocar* recording 16.8mpg overall – almost 2mpg better than previously – and nearly 20mpg on a 'long and gentle cross-country trip'. This writer went one better when convoying a Land-Rover and trailer (carrying a Jaguar ancestor, incidentally, in the form of a 1931 Standard Swallow) on the M5 at a steady 30mph, some 32mpg being recorded with a factory test car. This particular example could not match *Autocar*'s top speed, however, resolutely refusing to indicate more than

120mph – but there was no denying that the increased 'zip' of the injected engine had turned the XJ6 into a real sports saloon once more.

Alas, sales of the XJ12 had been discontinued in the United States, largely due to its thirst for fuel knocking Jaguar's corporate consumption figure and incurring excessive 'gas guzzler' tax across the range. So when *Road & Track* tested a Series 3, it was the six-cylinder edition. 'It's a most exhilarating car to drive fast', was the journal's opinion, although puzzlement was expressed at some of the cosmetic and detail alterations as they sometimes seemed to be 'changes for the sake of change'. A sign of the times was *R&T*'s description of the 4.2-litre engine as 'big', though it and the 'exceptionally clean and neatly laid out' engine compartment were very much approved of. About the only drawback to the car, *R&T* felt, was the marque's mixed reputation for reliability and the quality of its dealerships. As for performance, considering the 'emission' version of the engine gave only 176bhp, the 0-60mph time of 10.6 seconds was good; top speed was given as 117mph at 5,000rpm.

Car and Driver were far less lukewarm in their appraisal of the Series 3, and as usual their (June 1980) road test was rich in simile; how about 'slick as the inside of Faye Dunaway's dressing gown' for a description of the XJ6? Or on a more literary bent, 'a Jaguar simply assumes a receptive and yet highly participatory role in the sensual and free-thinking act of travel . . .' But a more down-to-earth account of the car was included and most of the revisions to the specification were welcomed, including the new front seats, the cruise control, and 'the quality of everything from the map-light to the twin-cam engine'. The injected straight-six was considered so good that it was even wondered whether a V12 was necessary at all . . .

About the only lingering doubts concerned, as ever, Jaguar's reputation for unreliability (especially in its electrical equipment). 'A lot of this bad repute is myth . . . but it's a powerful myth, reinforced by just enough truth to keep it ever at the front of our minds. This is a damned shame, because it will keep large numbers of Americans from going out and sampling an XJ6 – surely one of the silkiest, most satisfying luxury cars available in this country.'

The popularity of the V12-engined XJs received a big boost on the arrival of the May head and the increased economy it brought. This is the XJ12 5.3HE with the new drilled wheels – the car also has the sunroof and headlamp wash/wipe.

The totally equipped Vanden Plas Daimler Double Six became the top of the new HE range.

However, a lot of people on the other side of the Atlantic were hard at work to eliminate this side of the equation, because, towards the end of April 1980, Jaguar was given its own Chairman once more. Michael Edwardes, who had been charged with rescuing BL from the mess created – or at least continued – first by Lord Stokes and then by Sir Don Ryder, had offered one John Egan the job. At 40, Egan had more than proved his worth as both engineer and administrator, first in the oil industry, then with AC-Delco, then Unipart (which he created for BL), and subsequently as part of Massey-Ferguson's top management team.

On his arrival at Browns Lane and the hallowed office of Sir William Lyons above Jaguar's main entrance, overlooking the flag-poled front courtyard, John Egan quickly learned of the poor morale and of the production problems, talking not just to senior executives, but also to departmental managers, union officials and the workforce itself. He also made sure he learned about Jaguar's past, too, and how things had been done in Sir William's day. In short, he absorbed the atmosphere of the place and rapidly confirmed his belief that Jaguar wasn't simply the 'big luxury car' division of BL, but a very special entity of its own, and that this 'spirit of Jaguar' needed to survive and flourish if the whole company was to do the same.

He also read the same road-test reports relayed to you in these chapters, and saw that, especially in the United States, the general theme running through them all was admiration bordering on adulation – but with a sting in the tail in that the journals couldn't bring themselves to wholeheartedly recommend the purchase of a Jaguar because of tales told of things ceasing to work or falling off. John Egan's response was to launch what he called a 'crusade on excellence', pin-pointing the worst problem areas on the cars and allocating them to various committees to sort out, with the board itself taking on the 12 worst areas.

Communicating with the workforce came high on Egan's list of priorities, too, and special video presentations were given to 200 people at a time with the theme on quality. From one of these early shows came the idea of 'Quality Circles', which then met weekly all over the factory and allowed everyone to make suggestions on how things could be done better and what

An interesting newcomer for 1984 was the Jaguar Sovereign, although the type had previously replaced the Daimler on continental markets. This is the Jaguar Sovereign HE, the V12 version.

The Jaguar Sovereign has also appeared in six-cylinder form for those who want a fuller specification but without the expense of a 12-cylinder engine.

Interior of the Jaguar Sovereign 4.2; note the veneer door cappings. Footwell rugs are also featured, but were still in their bags in the boot when this brand-new car was photographed!

components were causing problems and why. Outside suppliers were sorted-out with ruthless energy (between 60% and 80% of the cars' reliability problems were 'bought in', with some components having a failure rate of 50%!) and given six months to clean up their acts or get out. Most did so, though a few lost their contracts. Sacrifices were called for, too, and the workforce was reduced from 10,500 to 6,500.

Gradually, and with much effort, the situation was pulled round; constant comparisons with BMW and Mercedes cars showed that the 'quality gap' was decreasing, and backed up by some imaginative advertising, which stressed the 'pursuit of perfection', sales began to pick up dramatically at home and overseas. North America, in particular, was receptive to the improved breed of cat, and there began a succession of record sales to the States – from an annual total of around 4,500 cars in the dark days of 1979, to a projected 18,200 for 1984!

The important European market wasn't neglected, either, and a wholly-owned subsiduary, Jaguar Deutschland GmbH, started business on January 1, 1984. As Germany accounts for 60% of all luxury saloons sold in Europe it was imperative that

Jaguar improved its fairly miserable share of the market there, especially as Europe as a whole took a mere 17% of total Jaguar sales in 1982; by taking its cars away from BL distributors, Jaguar secured better control of marketing, and it emphasized the special nature of the product. The XJ-S racing programme (see Chapter 6) was of course a very important part of the European sales drive.

Meanwhile, the range was being refined and reprofiled. The shortsighted BL policy of raising the price of Jaguars and Daimlers at every opportunity ceased, and in October 1980 Jaguar hit back at low-priced BMW and Mercedes models with a revised-specification XJ 3.4 Series 3 – an all-important move to lower the threshold of Jaguar ownership. Over £500 was lopped from the price of the 3.4, which now came out at £12,750, or almost exactly the same as a Mercedes 280E; but little in its specification was sacrificed to bring about this reduction, just a cheaper radio and manual aerial being fitted.

As before, cloth upholstery was standard on the 3.4 (but leather was an extra-cost option); so was central locking and the five-speed gearbox – the Borg-Warner Model 65 automatic

The 1984-model Daimler 4.2 has a similar level of trim to the Jaguar version. Note the extra veneer on doors and centre console; this car is a comparatively rare manual version.

transmission cost an additional £200. If you wanted such luxuries as air-conditioning, electric seat adjustment, electric sunroof, headlamp wash/wipe and alloy road wheels, these and much more could be specified at extra cost.

Across the range for 1981, the 6,000-mile service was extended to 7,500 miles and the 12,000-mile service to 15,000 miles. Previously, in May 1980, the 3,000-mile check had been dispensed with, and the North American service schedules had already been based on 7,500-mile intervals for a while before.

The big news during 1981 was the arrival of the 'HE' engine in July, standardized in all the V12 cars – a full description of this development is given in the XJ-S chapter, but the benefits accruing from the new version's greater efficiency were equally apparent in the saloon, even though the sporting model seemed to get the lion's share of publicity at the time. Going on 'official' figures, the HE saloons now gave 15mpg on the urban cycle, compared with only 12.5 previously, while at a steady 56mph, 26.8mpg was produced against 21.2; and at a constant 75mph, the cars returned 21.5, a 3.3mpg improvement. Jaguar did not omit to point out that the nearest comparable Mercedes, the 500

SEL saloon, could only manage 14, 24.4 and 20.2mpg, respectively.

What this meant in practice was that a normally-driven XJ12 or Double Six would return a similar petrol consumption to that of the pre-injection six-cylinder Jaguars of a year or so previously, and an overall consumption of nearly 20mpg was within reach. The new gearing helped, too – the final-drive ratio for the 12-cylinder cars was now 2.88:1, which also raised the maximum speed to virtually 150mph. But it was the substantially decreased thirst that was the biggest weapon in the armoury Jaguar were using to win back sales for the 5.3-litre cars.

However, this factor was backed-up by a whole package aimed at luring the customer into trying the car – and it has long since been acknowledged by Jaguar dealers that so far as an XJ is concerned, driving is believing (one in four who drive, buy – an amazing percentage). For a start, the exclusivity of the XJ12 was emphasized by a range of colours unique to it, plus a chrome waistline moulding. Alloy wheels were standardized for the model (the same castings as previously, but now silver-enamelled all over), as were the electric sunroof, twin electrically controlled door mirrors, and the headlamp wash/wipe (with two new heavy-duty pumps). The wheels were now shod with 215/70 VR15 Dunlop D7 tyres, giving more precise roadholding, handling and straight-line steering 'feel' than the previous 205/70 covers, though unlike the XJ-S HE, the rim width stayed at 6 inches. To let the world know you were driving the latest model, the letters 'HE' replaced the '5.3' symbol on the bootlid.

Broadly speaking, the specification of the Daimler Double Six was uprated in a similar manner, though the alloy wheels were still an option – this was part of a deliberate policy to create a more distinctly different character for the Daimler, so instead of sporty wheels the Double Six was given electrically-operated height adjustment for the front seats, deep-pile rugs for the rear footwells, carpet extended onto the lower parts of the 'A' posts, detachable rear-seat headrests, and smooth instead of embossed leather seat centres. All aimed at promoting the 'luxury carriage' image of the Daimler.

This was taken to the greatest degree in the Double Six Vanden Plas, which had air-conditioning as standard, even more plush seating, lined inserts to the veneer door fillets, and other minor trim refinements; cruise control was also a standard fitment, and the same package came with the Daimler 4.2 Vanden Plas model. As for the six-cylinder cars generally, they'd already had their major mechanical upgrading with the introduction of fuel injection, and this time round nearly all the changes in that direction were confined to improvements in cooling. For the first time on a Jaguar six-cylinder road car, an oil cooler was fitted, while the radiator benefited from a larger, 18-inch, cooling fan of a type used on the V12 cars; this, as before, used a viscous coupling which allowed the fan to 'freewheel' at high revs, but it now carried a thermostatic device which controlled that slip in direct relationship to the coolant temperature.

Additionally, a larger, clear-plastic header tank (still remote) was positioned higher up in the engine bay for improved flow – it also ensured that the correct amount of coolant was always present, the previous tank sometimes giving false readings in that respect. Both six- and 12-cylinder cars now had low-maintenance batteries which needed only an annual check –

previously, the appetite for distilled water required checks of even weekly frequency on some cars!

One item welcomed by a large section of the motoring press and many drivers was the new gear selector fitted on all the automatic gearboxes across the range – the GM 400 on the V12s, and the Borg-Warner Model 66 (an updated version of the Model 65) on the 'sixes'. This now included a detent to stop the inadvertent selection of Neutral (or even Reverse!) from Drive, and the deletion of the one which (quite unnecessarily) had previously featured between Drive and 2. A much more natural action was now possible when the selection of 2 was required, and there was no longer any need to glance at the selector on returning the lever to Drive in case one overshot into Neutral.

The five-speed manual gearbox, however, was the standard fitment on the 4.2, though most people chose the optional automatic. Leather upholstery continued as standard, cloth still being the option. Tinted glass, quartz halogen headlights, and a combined radio/cassette player were, along with the leather, items which set the 4.2 apart from the 3.4, which remained the lowest-price Jaguar – though it, too, included electric windows, central locking, childproof rear locks, adjustable lumbar support for the front seats, cubby hole light and door-open guard lights in its specification, along with the bigger-engined models. A new colour-keyed heel mat was fitted to the driver's side only on all cars (with the Jaguar name and symbol or Daimler script moulded in as appropriate), while unique to the Daimlers was the useful feature of a reversible bootmat, which had rubber on one side and carpet on the other.

These, then, were the cars that carried Jaguar through 1982, a year which saw virtually a doubling of sales in North America, and a renewed attack on other overseas markets – in April 1982 sales and marketing once more came under direct Jaguar control, one of the last major functions to do so (the parts operation alone were to remain with BL for a while longer). Headed by Neil Johnson, Australia, the Middle East and Japan were the immediate targets for the department, which also continued the aggressive campaign to improve the dealer network: 'As far as Jaguar is concerned, a bad dealer is worse than no dealer at all', said Johnson. Some 40 were given their marching orders and more went the same way subsequently when they showed no inclination to improve. Jaguar meant business!

In October 1982, Jaguar released details of their new European sales programme, along with news of the 1983 model range. This included some significant changes, most notable of which was the dropping of the Daimler name on the continental market. Daimlers represented but 22% of the company's European sales and tended to create confusion amongst customers (not the least in Germany, the home of Daimler-Benz), while concentrating on a single marque would simplify marketing and bring economies by way of rationalized sales literature and (eventually) parts. Instead, there was a new high-specification Jaguar, the Sovereign, which would soon become available on the home market, too.

On the existing line-up of Jaguars and Daimlers, nothing was dramatically changed for 1983, and only the XJ12 HE looked obviously different from the outside, thanks to new alloy road wheels of modern 'perforated' design (these could be ordered on 3.4 and 4.2 Jaguars for an extra £543; Daimlers retained the previous spoked alloy wheels, which were standard on the VDP 5.3 car). There were detail alterations, however, the leaping cat wing badges being restyled, the silver-on-black six-cylinder-type grille badge being commonized on all Jaguars, and the chromium bonnet strip on Daimlers being deleted, thanks to a small modification to the Daimler grille. The Jaguar 3.4 now carried a single coachline, while the two larger-engined models displayed twin fine-line coachlines; the Daimlers also carried a bright chromium side moulding. The eagle-eyed might also have spotted that 1983-model XJ6 3.4s left the factory with quartz halogen headlights, which meant that the entire range was now so equipped.

Improvements inside the cars were a little more obvious, and the most significant of these was the new centre console; the upper part was of vacuum-formed plastic and included the switch panel and a storage tray, and both upper and lower switch panels were finished in gloss figured walnut veneer (Jaguar models) or gloss burr walnut veneer (Daimler models). The analogue clock or trip computer was moved to the upper console and new marque badges were positioned in the centre of the lower console.

Both Jaguars and Daimlers now had rear passenger consoles finished in black (previously seen only on Daimlers), and for the driver there was a thicker-rimmed steering wheel, meeting a minor but fairly consistent criticism of the previous wheel. Small changes also occurred to gear levers and selectors (the latter moved slightly rearwards for easier access to controls), there was a relocated rheostat knob, a new horn-push pad for Daimlers, and a new panel with black-grained finish carrying the radio and heater/air-conditioning functions. Seating was improved by internal stiffening of the front seats, while a new fine-line-patterned Raschelle material was adopted for the cloth-trimmed XJ6 3.4 (this upholstery being optional on the Jaguar XJ6 and XJ12).

Headlining colour was now standardized as Limestone, whatever trim colour was specified, there was more wood veneer on Daimler and VDP doors (Daimlers were also fitted with a bootlid liner), while 'in response to customer demand' the attache-case-style tool kit made a reappearance on all models. Mechanically, nothing significant was altered for 1983, though of course the ceaseless 'pursuit of perfection' continued, resulting in the usual minor but useful improvements to the unseen components of the cars.

When the time came to announce the 1984 model cars, Jaguar

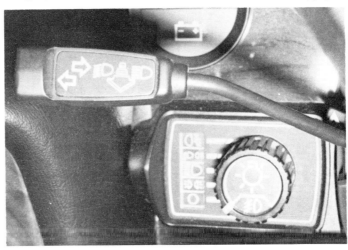

Light controls and minor instruments on the 1984 Jaguar; the latter are identified from symbols instead of words.

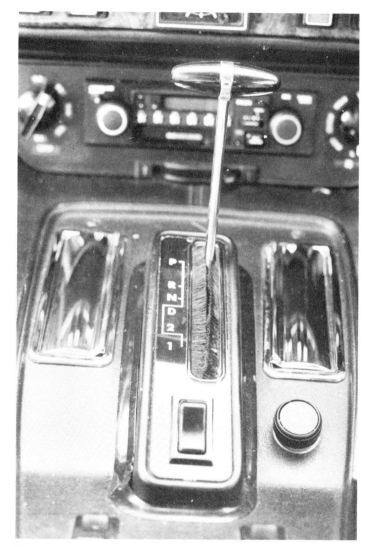

The latest automatic gear selector with the revised quadrant, allowing unobstructed changes between 'D' and '2', but with a detent to stop the inadvertent selection of neutral or reverse.

was in a bouyant mood; the XJ-S and XJR-5 racing programmes were beginning to bear fruit, the company was back in profit, sales were still escalating, and privatization was now a question of 'when' not 'if'; but in this somewhat heady atmosphere it was still up to Jaguar's engineers to further enhance the XJ range, even if much of their time had to be spent on developing XJ40, its successor.

The changes this time round were, however, not merely limited to improvements for their own sake, but centred around a realignment of the range which had already begun the year before. Broadly speaking, this meant giving the Daimlers a more exclusive, luxury image – though conversely, it was acknowledged that some Jaguar owners, too, wanted a higher level of sumptuousness. The result was a total range of six cars, of which just two were Daimlers.

New to the home market was the Jaguar Sovereign, in essence a high-specfication version of the XJ6 4.2 (which continued). For a start it was given the new perforated alloy wheels and electric remote-control door mirrors, while inside were electric rise and fall seats, trip computer, rear head restraints, seatbelts and reading lights, passenger footwell rugs, air-conditioning and a carpeted boot. It cost £18,495 against the normal 4.2's £15,997, but this was almost £1,000 less than the former Vanden Plas 4.2, despite even more equipment. All these features – plus cruise control, headlamp wash/wipe and a more expensive stereo radio/cassette player – were incorporated in a 12-cylinder version, too, the new Jaguar Sovereign HE. This replaced the XJ12, and while at £20,995 it was over £1,000 dearer, with all its equipment it was more fairly comparable to the 1983 model Daimler Double Six HE, which had retailed for £21,372. Jaguar's competitive pricing policy continued with the XJ6 3.4 which, remarkably, cost no more than it had done in 1980; additionally, keeping the price to £13,951 meant that it fell below the £14,000 business-car taxation bracket. Likewise, the XJ6 4.2 represented excellent value for money, being only 1% more expensive than in 1980, whereas Jaguar were quick to point out – Mercedes and BMW equivalents had risen by 14%. All this was made possible by greater efficiency on the shop floor, and of course by increased sales.

The only two Daimlers in the range (not counting the limousine), were the Daimler 4.2 and the Daimler Double Six;

For 1984 the XJ remained available with the 3.4-litre engine and was still priced below £14,000 in Great Britain.

at £22,946 and £26,965 they very much represented the top end, but included front foglamps, electric steel sunroof, spoked alloy wheels, bucket-style rear seats, walnut door casing inserts and cruise control as standard. All this meant a very logical disposition of models, with Daimler firmly at the summit and a good price/specification range of Jaguars for the customer to choose from. In the United States, incidentally, there were no extras as such – every car came 'fully loaded', as the expression goes, which made the cars better value than might have at first appeared; BMW and Mercedes buyers had to watch the cost of options rather closely if they were not to end up spending rather more than they intended . . .

It was in January 1984 that *Autocar* published their road test of what had become a rare and (so far as the press were concerned) elusive Jaguar variant – the manual Series 3 XJ6 saloon. This model had been absent from Jaguar's road-test fleet and no independent journal had managed to borrow one for long enough to take figures, inevitably giving rise to rumours that the 'Rover' five-speed box wasn't capable of handling the fuel-injected engine's torque and could be unreliable. While only a

handful of customers requested the manual gearbox (about 15% of the 1983 production), few problems were in fact reported, and certainly nothing untoward happened during *Autocar*'s tenure of their five-speeder.

The twin benefits of the manual gearbox were economy and the ability to use the XK engine's great flexibility – it was possible to take acceleration figures in top gear from 10mph, and indeed *Autocar* used the same Series 3 to re-enact the first Land's End-to-John o' Groats run of 1911 using top gear only (successfully accomplished – including all starts – in fifth gear, if at some cost in clutch linings!). Compared to the previously tested automatic Series 3 4.2, petrol consumption had gone down from 16.8mpg to 18.3mpg, with 23-25mpg available on long runs.

Acceleration was also improved, notably from a standing start in the lower speed ranges, where the 0-60mph time dropped from 10 to 8.6 seconds. As for a comparison between the old manual/overdrive gearbox and the new five-speed box, it was thought that the extra gear did not really match the long-legged cruising ability bestowed by the Laycock 'fifth', the 3.31 axle

77

The 3.4-litre XK engine in 1984 trim; note the V12-type oil filler cap, adopted on six-cylinder cars some time previously, and the heat shroud on the exhaust manifolds.

Mainstay of the Jaguar range from 1984 has been – as always – the 4.2-litre car, now faster and more reliable than ever with its refined injection engine.

The Daimler Double Six (though not with the VDP label any more) in 1984 form; along with the Jaguar 5.3, it is still one of the world's best cars.

The V12 HE power unit, to 1984 UK-market specification – 300bhp, 145mph and, with a gentle approach to the throttle, perhaps 16mpg.

ratio fitted being too low; the 3.07 ratio could be supplied to special order, though, which would have helped. As it was, at the conservative red-line of 5,000rpm the speeds available in the intermediates were 35, 55, 83 and 116mph, with 131mph coming up in top. However, fifth gear represented only a 10% overdrive, and *Autocar* reckoned that the car could pull something more like 20%.

The installation of the gearbox was successful in general, except that the pedal positions were not considered ideal and the clutch was heavy; also, the XK engine's top-end vibrations showed up more obviously with the manual gearbox, and wheelspin starts provoked the rear subframe's tendency to judder alarmingly (but such antics were seldom indulged in by owner-drivers, and the few that did could always avail themselves of Forward Engineering's anti-tramp brackets!). Because of this, *Autocar* considered that the car 'shows signs of something rare in present Jaguars – insufficient development', though still rating it 'a very desirable machine'.

Nevertheless, the five-speed XJ6 4.2 was undoubtedly the most 'sporting' of the Series 3 saloons, inasmuch as such a term could be applied to the range. Without a torque converter, response to the throttle was crisp and immediate, and of course – unlike the automatic box – you could select exactly the right gear for the circumstances. In particular, the 'acceleration gap'

Accompanying Richard Noble's world land speed record-breaking Thrust 2 was a specially prepared Series 3 XJ12; it now resides at Silverstone, having taken over most of the fire-fighting duties performed by the now-elderly Series 1 pre-production XJ12 used previously.

suffered even by the V12 cars between 30mph and 50mph (due to the refusal of the automatic box to kick-down into first above the former speed) was abolished, making the manual Jaguar a quicker and safer car for overtaking slow traffic.

Sentiment apart, for all *practical* purposes the Series 3 Jaguars were the best of the XJ saloons; they were quieter, less thirsty and faster than their Series 1 and 2 predecessors, and they had many more useful items as standard equipment. In short, they were easier to live with as a 'working' car. About the only area in which the Series 3 was not noticeably superior to the original Series 1 of 1968 lay in its handling, not so much because of the longer wheelbase, but more because damping remained on the soft side. The XJ of the mid-1980s was built for comfort, not for outright speed along a twisty 'B' road. But there always has to be a ride/handling compromise, and with their Series 3 Jaguar still managed to get their sums more nearly right than almost anybody else.

Future Jaguars will be lighter, more responsive, and a lot more economical; but the XJ range will still be regarded as the pinnacle of Jaguar's big-car era by most people. Particularly in the case of the 147mph XJ12, such magnificent motoring will perhaps never be seen again, even from Browns Lane.

CHAPTER 6

The XJ-S range

V12 express and AJ6 pathfinder

The XJ-S has aroused more comment and criticism than almost any other car from the Lyons stable – with the possible exception of the original SS1 of 1931! Its styling was controversial and the whole concept of the car – a 2-plus-2 measuring almost 16ft stem to stern and with a 14mpg thirst – was questionable to many observers. Yet, despite a shaky start and an even shakier period in the late 1970s, the XJ-S has become one of Jaguar's most successful sporting models with, at the time of writing, over a year's waiting list for some versions.

The biggest disadvantage the XJ-S suffered at the beginning was from preconceptions. Although rumours from Coventry hinted to the contrary, expectations were high that Jaguar would produce a true successor to the E-type, namely a 'real' sports car of relatively compact dimensions and available in open as well as closed form. Instead, Jaguar chose to follow another branch of the evolutionary tree, and what emerged at the Frankfurt show in September 1975 was fairly radically different – a large, luxury GT with no soft-top option. Worse, its styling, far from being the usual Jaguar triumph, was certainly not universally acclaimed. It was also a very expensive motor car; for the first time a Jaguar cost as much as a Ferrari . . .

Yet given the role which Jaguar had determined for it, the XJ-S was a superb performer in virtually every department, and even those who were critical of its styling were usually won over to the car after a spell at the wheel. With such outstanding performance, such refinement and such poise there to enjoy, what did a slightly oversize bodyshell and possibly quirky rear-end styling matter? As a Grand Tourer, the XJ-S had rivals, but no equals; no other car in the world could be driven as fast, as smoothly and as quietly over long distances. A lot could be forgiven in exchange for qualities like those!

The XJ-S story began in the late 1960s when serious thought was first given to an E-type replacement. Even then, there was no indication that Jaguar ever contemplated its traditional return to basics when designing a new sports car – while the E-type had reverted to an XK 120-type strict two-seater format, instead of continuing the 2-plus-2 XK 150 theme, XJ27 (as the new car was coded) very definitely carried on from where the 2-plus-2 long-wheelbase E-type left off. This went hand-in-hand with the decision to use the recently introduced XJ6 saloon as a base, which rather determined its minimum size and weight, while the 'sporting' aspects of the new car were further pushed back when, in common with most other manufacturers, Jaguar believed that regulations would soon outlaw all open cars in the United States; as it happened, these proposals were scotched in 1974, but by that time, of course, the XJ-S was on the point of announcement.

The first prototype XJ27 was built around 1970 on a 102in wheelbase version of the (normally 108in) XJ saloon floorpan; styling was in the hands of Malcolm Sayer, and his ideas for the new GT car differed radically from those expressed in his previous sports car designs, the C, D and E-types. Gone were most of the beautifully blended curves, replaced by a mainly flat bonnet, chopped-off rear end, and slab sides. But the most distinctive feature of the new design was, of course, the 'flying buttress' treatment aft of the side windows.

These 'wings' swept down from the roof and, curving gently inwards, blended into the tail and rear wings, almost enclosing

Beginnings of the XJ-S shape can be seen in this *circa* 1964 Jaguar saloon prototype, mainly in the disposition of the headlights and the inward-sloping front wings.

Malcolm Sayer was preoccupied with flying buttresses early on, and they cropped up on a purely experimental E-type 2-plus-2 update in the mid-1960s.

An advanced styling buck of the XJ-S with all major features of the eventual car present. Note, however, the bright strip in the bumper, the horizontally lined finisher behind the side windows and the opening roof, none of which appeared on the production XJ-S.

Former world champion (and ex-Jaguar driver) Phil Hill chats to retired Jaguar Chairman Lofty England about the new XJ-S; behind is the last true Jaguar sports car, the Series 3 V12 E-type roadster.

The original XJ-S; its styling was controversial and not instantly liked by everyone, particularly the rear-end treatment.

the near-vertical rear window. Almost certainly they were inspired by the Italian coachbuilding fashions prevailing in the late 1960s, and perhaps in particular by the 206 and 246GT Dino Ferraris, with their Pininfarina-designed bodywork developed from a styling exercise by the same house and exhibited – complete with sports-racing-style flying buttresses – at the Paris show of 1965. Sayer was obviously very taken with this feature at the time, and had even incorporated them on a purely experimental mock-up on the 2-plus-2 E-type back in 1968. But on the XJ-S they were also intended to be functional – Doug Thorpe, Director of Styling at Jaguar until recently, recalls how Sayer explained to him that the 'twist' of the buttresses towards the rear of the car, unique to the XJ-S, were for an aerodynamic spillage and were entirely intentional on his part.

Tragically, Malcolm Sayer died in 1970, though by this time the basic design and structure of the bodyshell had been finalized; Doug Thorpe and his fellow stylists then took up the work. Thorpe didn't entirely agree with some of the car's features, including the flying buttresses, but it was too late for major changes and they could only influence detail aspects of the design. Possibly it was this involuntary transfer of styling responsibility which provides some substance to the 'designed by committee' taunt occasionally levelled at the XJ-S.

Some aspects of the car's design were influenced by the legislative requirements of the North American market – one of the reasons for the demise of the E-type, the fuel tank of which could not have met the Federal 30mph rear-impact test scheduled for 1976. The XJ-S had its tank positioned across the rear suspension, well out of harm's way, and the short but deep boot was particularly strong. American-made piston-type Menasco struts filled with silicon wax carried front and rear bumpers made from deformable plastic, which met the 5mph no-damage impact test – unlike on the saloons, this arrangement was standard on home-market cars as well, and it was very effective.

While the bodyshell was based on that of the saloon, there were substantial changes. The shorter wheelbase was achieved by moving the rear suspension assembly – and thus the rear bulkhead – forwards, while at the front, the shell was strengthened by increasing the triangulation of the front bulkhead and engine bay sides up to where they met the windscreen pillars. The shell was mainly built in 22-gauge steel rather than the lighter 24-gauge more commonly used by car manufacturers, though this was shared by the saloon, too. The doors included anti-intrusion barriers and reinforced hinges as standard.

Total weight of the XJ-S shell was 720lb, a useful 100lb lighter than the long-wheelbase saloon's, and it incorporated

American export cars (both North and South) had what were derisively termed within the factory as 'glow-worm' headlamps, the low-wattage round lights being much less powerful than the specially designed Cibié units used on home-market cars. This example is being eagerly examined at a Brazilian Jaguar Driver's Club event.

everything Jaguar had learned about noise suppression – the engine bay was shaped to deflect noise from the interior, and the front bulkhead used the same built-in plug-and-socket electrical connections as the saloons to avoid grommeted holes. Extensive use was made of sound-deadening materials (lined with heat-reflecting aluminium on the front bulkhead and parts of the engine compartment sides) and even such as the alloy drain tube for the air intake plenum chamber was broken by rubber sections to avoid transmitting engine and road noise.

The XJ-S used the same basic front and rear suspension assemblies as the saloon, the difference of 2cwt in weight being compensated for by bringing the front spring rates down from 92 to 90lb/in at the front and from 154 to 125lb/in at the rear. Unique to the XJ-S was the rear anti-roll bar (of 0.562in diameter) fitted to increase roll stiffness; at the front, the latest specification XJ12 anti-roll bar was featured (slightly thicker

than before) but at 3.5 degrees the castor angle was a degree more than the saloon's. All this was the result of much experimentation by chassis engineer Jim Randle (now Jaguar's Director of Engineering) under the watchful eye of Bob Knight; the aim was to maintain a supremely good ride, but provide the XJ-S driver with slightly more sporting handling.

Brakes were the same as for the XJ saloon, namely 11.18in ventilated discs with four-pot calipers at the front, and 10.38in plain discs at the rear. Wheels were XJ12 alloy-type, fitted with a new steel-braced Dunlop radial tyre designated the Formula 70 SP Super Sport; still 205-section, it was claimed to provide even better wet-road grip and improved traction.

The magnificent V12 light-alloy engine was to the same fuel injected specification as in the latest XJ 5.3 saloons, giving around 287bhp, and it drove through a Borg-Warner Model 12 automatic gearbox – though, to the delight of the few

Some minor controls were common to the XJ saloons, but the instruments were new. Absence of veneer tended to make the interior a little austere. This is a manual-gearbox car, the only V12 Jaguar to be released as such.

The much more common automatic car (below left) had a conventional gear selector, flanked by ashtrays. Air-conditioning controls bracket the radio. Rear accommodation (below) wasn't exactly generous, and for a 2-plus-2 the overall size of the car was called into question by some. One adult sitting transversely could be quite comfortable, however.

With the fuel tank set across the rear axle (probably to avoid possible collision/fire damage, which had already involved BL in law-suits with the XJ saloon), the XJ-S boot is deep and short, rather than shallow and long, as with the saloon. The upright spare wheel sits next to the battery.

enthusiasts who ordered one, the XJ-S was also available with the four-speed manual gearbox of the type used on the V12 E-type, suitably modified to take the additional power of the injected engine. In either case, the power went to the road wheels via a Salisbury final-drive unit incorporating a 3.07:1 Powr-Lok differential. No overdrive was available, of course, but Jaguar were still developing an electrically controlled two-speed axle with the intention of offering it on the XJ-S – and in the impressive bank of warning lights on the dash, a slot was left empty for it . . .

The interior of the XJ-S represented something of a surprise to anyone expecting XJ saloon-type appointments. Here, at least, Jaguar had continued one of their sports car traditions – that established in 1957 with the coming of the XK 150 of abolishing wood veneer in their sporting model. As a consequence, the XJ-S was given a vacuum-formed plastic facia in black, a black instrument panel and all-vinyl door trims.

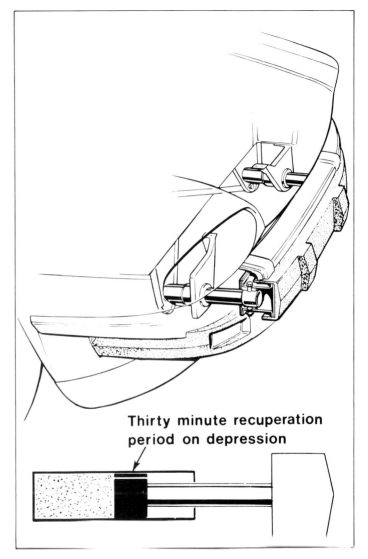

Thirty minute recuperation period on depression

The highly effective 5mph-impact-absorbing bumpers, which are standard on all XJ-S models.

87

The Jaguar V12 engine as installed in the XJ-S; the combination has produced one of the most impressive Grand Touring cars ever made. The air-conditioning pump can be seen in the centre of the 'V'.

Connolly hide and thick-pile carpeting did little to offset the rather sombre and even slightly austere look, especially when the interior colour was black.

Nor did the instruments get universal acclaim – while the 160mph speedometer and 7,000rpm rev-counter retained the clear, white-lettering-on-black-face style, they were contained within rather cheap-looking cowls, and the secondary instruments (water, oil, fuel and voltage) were of a vertical drum type; of sophisticated design, using three opposing coils, they were quick-acting and more accurate than before, but their unconventional appearance didn't always bring a rapturous response from owners. Above the instruments was a panel of warning lights which, in almost Citroen fashion, indicated faults in braking and lighting circuits – amber meant investigate when convenient, red meant check at once.

XJ-type stalks controlled wipers, indicators and headlight dip/flash, and while the steering wheel retained the same 15½in diameter as the saloons, it was given a new, leather-bound rim. The XJ's umbrella-type handbrake was swopped for one which lay outboard of the driver's seat, and which after being applied dropped down to floor level again, out of the way.

The car's seats were all-new. Big, bucket-type featured in the front, fully reclined and with new two-section cushions – a 'soft' centre and a harder surround, designed to provide lateral support by gently locating the occupant once he or she had sat down. Individual-style rear seats were fitted, separated by a tray (containing the rear seat belt buckles) over the prop-shaft tunnel; beautifully trimmed, they could accommodate two adults, but only if those in the front didn't mind pulling their seats forward quite a way – there was, after all, 5in less room than in the saloon. The car was thus more fairly described as a 2-plus-2 than a genuine four-seater; headroom as well as knee-room was another limiting factor.

The XJ-S was very definitely a luxury car: air conditioning was standard, as were electric windows, central locking, a radio and even five separate interior lights; it was very much a 'total package' designed to take over the flagship role from the XJ12 as the top Jaguar, which was perhaps not quite the original intention back in 1970. However, when plans for an open version (coded XJ28) had to be dropped, refinement and

XJ-S fortunes fluctuated until the arrival of the HE version, then demand soon outstripped supply. New wheels, bright bumper trim and – above all, perhaps – the 'HE' badge distinguished the new, more efficient version of the car.

comfort gradually usurped outright sporting appeal as the main design priority, and it is probably true to say that the XJ-S's character underwent a definite change of emphasis between the prototype and production stages.

So much for the car's specification – how did it all work on the road? In a word, superlatively. The XJ-S was usefully quicker and tauter-handling than the 12-cylinder Jaguar saloons, yet retained their by now legendary disdain for poor road surfaces and their almost complete imperviousness to mechanical, road and (to a slightly lesser extent) wind noise. The XJ-S flowed rather than rode down highways and byways, wafted from corner to corner by the discreet might of its superb – and imperturbable – power unit. Where speed limits and traffic allowed, 120 to 130mph was a usable and unflustered cruising speed, obtained in less than half-a-minute from standstill. While by no means faultless, the XJ-S quickly proved itself to be a car which elevated the term 'Grand Tourer' onto an altogether higher plane; it had been deliberately pitched at an entirely different segment of the high-performance market to the E-type, challenging cars like the 450 SLC Mercedes (hence its

gauntlet-throwing debut at Frankfurt), or even the Urraco or Dino, and for sheer long-distance, high-speed travel it appeared to be a match for any of them.

The hard facts – plus the usual subjective opinion – were soon supplied by the motoring press when they got their hands and stopwatches on press cars. In Britain, *Autocar* found that its manual version reached 60mph in 6.9 seconds and 100mph in only 11 seconds more, and recorded a maximum of 153mph. Despite performance-testing, a fuel consumption of 15.4mpg was recorded overall, and it was thought that 20mpg was within reach, given gentle driving over a longish journey – if so, fuel injection had certainly brought its benefits to the V12.

Motor were unable to carry out a maximum speed check on their manual XJ-S, but recorded marginally better acceleration figures, 100mph arriving in 16.2 instead of 16.9 seconds. The considerably poorer figure of 12.8mpg overall and the (projected) 'touring' mpg of 14.4 which *Motor* obtained do tally more closely than *Autocar*'s mpg figures with those obtained by owners of pre-HE cars, though 16 to 17mpg was quite feasible on a long run if the driver could resist using the silky surge of acceleration at every opportunity.

Both journals considered the steering to be on the light side, but were not over-critical of it; *Motor's* testers commented on the slight tendency of the car to 'float' over undulations taken at speed – a feature of the XJ saloons, too, and due to Jaguar

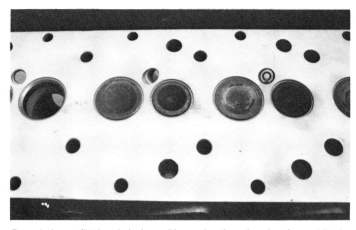

From being a flat-head design with combustion chamber formed in the piston (above), the V12 engine went over to a swirl-inducing chamber in the cylinder head when the May principle was adopted.

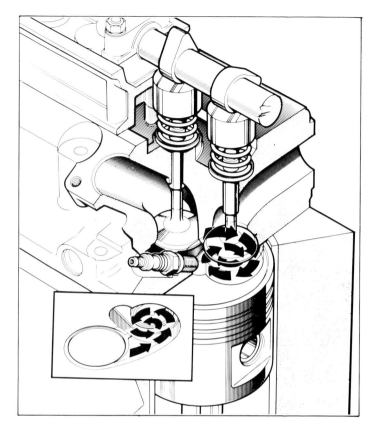

This diagram shows how the mixture enters from the inlet valve on the left, then is swirled into a chamber around the exhaust valve and sparking plug by the compression stroke. Inset is an underside view of the swirl pattern.

placing ride marginally over handling when it came to suspension settings. Otherwise, the car received the usual lavish praise for its 'exemplary' handling and 'remarkable' ride. Both magazines considered that for carrying large adults, the rear seats were for occasional use only – though *Motor* pointed out that the Aston Martin V8 and the Jensen Interceptor were equally at fault in this direction.

As indicated, both these test cars were fitted with the manual

Almost as important as the engine modifications were the changes to the interior of the XJ-S – at last, with glossy elm veneer and all-leather trim, it looked the high-speed luxury tourer it was.

Rear seats now included seat-belts, though as the bodyshell remained unaltered there still wasn't a great deal of room.

gearbox. This was a development of the four-speed all-synchromesh box introduced in 1964, and while it was reliable, by 1975 it had fallen a little behind the best; both *Motor* and *Autocar* commented on the stickiness of the change, and the former, too, on the comparative heaviness of the clutch (which needed a 38lb push).

But it was this transmission that enabled the smoothness, flexibility and response of the V12 engine to be savoured to the full, and *Autocar* recounted the 'top gear starting' feat, whereby you placed the lever in top, switched on, engaged the starter, and allowed the engine to pick up and accelerate all the way to 140mph without touching the clutch, in just under 70 seconds . . . 'Such flexibility has been the goal of engine designers since the beginning of the internal combustion engine' said the road-test report.

The alternative was the Model 12 automatic box, which most customers specified – more, in fact, than even Jaguar seem to have originally anticipated. It was well suited to the smooth effortlessness of the car, but it had some shortcomings when asked to perform in a sporting manner, and it was no

91

The XJ-S HE in 1984; note the 'antique'-finish bonnet badge and body stripes.

The 1984 car from the rear; the wheel rim width is now 6½in, and 215-section tyres are fitted. The current range of paint colours are very attractive, and somehow those flying buttresses don't look bad after all . . .

The first open Jaguar since 1975 – the XJ-SC. From windscreen forward the car is unaltered, however.

The SC with roof panels detached and the rear hood stowed under its envelope. Badging denotes the body style and engine size.

coincidence that all of Jaguar's early press road-test cars were released in manual form only. The Borg-Warner box often proved reluctant to change down, was a bit slow off the mark from standstill, and was generally lazy in the way it performed, irritatingly so to the keen driver. However, in more relaxed conditions it was perfectly adequate and it suited the majority of buyers, who were more 'executive' than 'sporting'. There were the usual first and second gear holds, but using the quadrant manually resulted in only fractions of seconds being saved on acceleration.

The XJ-S received the same rather mixed reception in the United States as it had in Europe, with some considering its appearance a bit too Transatlantic, rather too much like such home-based offerings as the Camaro, GM's response to the Mustang (actually, the XJ-S was 4in smaller in length and the same in width – but in the large expanse of bonnet and sloping roofline there were definite similarities). Likewise, the interior was sometimes a disappointment: 'pure Pinto', said *Car & Driver*, with regret, hankering after the saloons' wood dashboard. Everyone acknowledged the car's ability, though:

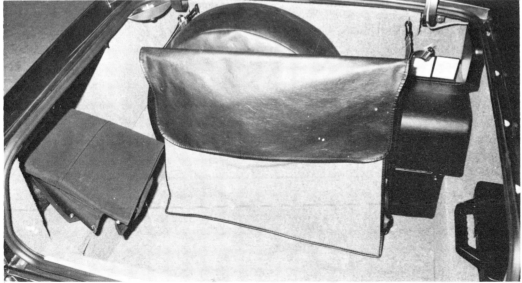

A short gear lever controls a Getrag five-speed box; this car (above left) is fitted with a trip computer which can give instant or cumulative readouts of fuel consumption, average speed, elapsed time, etc. There are no rear seats in the SC (above), but instead, two lockers and map or magazine containers.

Lift-out roof sections of the SC are carried in a bag when not in use, as is the cover on the left. Note the attache-case tool-kit on the right.

The XJ-S 3.6 has normal closed XJ-S bodywork and less extensive equipment than the cabriolet, but of course it is powered by the AJ6 engine driving through a five-speed manual gearbox.

'It's more than a little eerie', recounted *Road Test* magazine, almost in awe. 'It never ruffled its feathers, never tried to turn around and snap. It just flexed its broad shoulders and *worked*.' Or, as Patrick Bedard wrote in *Car & Driver*: 'The XJ-S is a dark and mysterious product of England's tortured auto industry, fantastically over-qualified for today's driving conditions . . .'

Cars destined for North America looked very similar to their European-market kin, the one big distinguishing feature being the four separate GEC tungsten headlights, instead of the advanced and highly efficient Cibié streamlined halogen units, this because of rather silly Federal restrictions on wattage. Opinions vary as to which was *visually* better; as a design exercise, a European four-headlight version using Cibié 5¾in units was later produced by Jaguar's experimental shop, but it was not well received by the management and was never adopted for production.

More seriously, perhaps, detoxing equipment under the bonnet took its toll on brake horsepower; while an air injection pump was standardized on European cars too, Federal cars had exhaust gas recirculation, an anti-run-on valve, an evaporative emissions carbon cannister for the fuel tank, and a catalytic reactor serving each bank of cylinders. Power went down to 244bhp at 5,250rpm and the 40bhp drop affected acceleration to 60mph by around a second, and to 100mph by nearer 4 seconds, despite a lower (3.31:1) final-drive ratio. Economy wasn't helped by all this, either.

Visually, the XJ-S changed less year-to-year than the Jaguar saloons, possibly because (as Doug Thorpe once remarked to me) the overall shape of the car did not lend itself to a major facelift. So throughout its life there have only been what amount to detail changes, the first batch arriving in 1977. Amongst these was a significant under-the-bonnet improvement, however, with the substitution in April of the GM 400 gearbox for the Borg-Warner Model 12. This was in parallel with the saloons, and produced a better response, though it still left an annoying 'performance gap' around 35 to 50mph as the box still refused to kick down into first above about 28mph.

Partly, this may have been an intentional safety factor to prevent the inexperienced getting themselves into trouble accelerating hard out of a slippery corner, but it seems that the

Swiss are really to blame! All new cars sold there have to pass a noise test, and for the V12 Jaguars to do so meant preventing a full-throttle kick-down into first at less than 35mph or so; for the same reason it's not possible to select first manually above around 28mph. It was not practical to calibrate gearboxes on cars bound for other markets separately, so the XJ-S (and the XJ12) retains this diminished pick-up in this rather vital overtaking speed range.

Visual changes arrived in the autumn of 1977 and the 1978-model XJ-S swopped its black-finished radiator grille for a bright-finished one, black also being banished from the bootlid's rear panel to be replaced by a body-colour panel. The central door pillar, however, adopted a matt-black finish, and inside, the instrument bezels lost their silver surrounds. November 1977 saw the demise of the two-door coupe, incidentally, leaving the XJ-S to enter 1978 in an undisputed position as Jaguar's sporting machine.

The year 1979 was notable mostly for the demise of the manual option for the XJ-S. Demand was simply not high enough to justify retaining the facility on the production line, and midway during the year the four-speeder was dropped from the range; for the record, the last production manual XJ-S was finished in Squadron Blue and carried the VIN number (Vehicle Identification Number) JNAEW1 AC 101814, though it is believed that at least two further manual XJ-Ss were completed to special order afterwards.

During 1979 and 1980 the XJ-S was rather overshadowed by the introduction of the new Series 3 range of saloons, and there was no distinct 1980 model as such. Instead, further efforts were made to improve economy pending the introduction of the radical new 'May' cylinder heads, which had been under development since 1976.

These mid-1980 interim changes centred around the adoption of the latest Lucas/Bosch digital electronic fuel injection and a rise in compression ratio to 10:1, which in practice decreased fuel consumption by a couple of mpg overall. They also increased the power to 300bhp at 5,400rpm and peak torque to 318lb/ft at 3,900rpm. In the United States, improvement was even more marked, thanks to substituting a three-way converter for the previous air injection and exhaust gas recirculation anti-emissions gear; this raised US-specification cars from 244 to 262bhp – this and more torque helped to knock a whole second off the 0-60mph time (now 7.8 seconds) despite a 3.07 instead of a 3.31:1 final-drive ratio. Fuel consumption dropped from around 12mpg to nearer 14mpg in normal driving conditions.

It is necessary to move forward to July 1981 for the next significant update for the XJ-S – and it was certainly needed because in the years since its launch sales had slumped, particularly during 1979, when Jaguar's American market went into something of a depression. All large, thirsty and expensive cars suffered, and the XJ-S was firmly amongst them, not helped by its reliability record and its high price on the North American market; the XJ12 actually had to be withdrawn. Production of the car dwindled and as the new decade arrived there were even whispers that the XJ-S would be discontinued altogether.

However, Michael May represented the cavalry on this occasion, along with John Egan's quality campaign. This independent Swiss engineer had circulated his ideas on what came to be known as the 'fireball' combustion chamber to the industry in 1976, and it wasn't long before Jaguar's power units division, then headed by Harry Mundy, saw the possibilities of applying it to their own V12 engine. Subsequently, Michael May brought his modified VW Passat to Browns Lane for inspection and demonstration; Jaguar were impressed and, somewhat desperate to salvage something from the substantial investment made in the facilities for making the V12 engine (at that time less than a quarter of all Jaguars made were 5.3s), a contract was signed.

Basically, the May combustion chamber is a split-level arrangement, with the inlet valve in a recessed collecting zone and the exhaust valve positioned higher up within the 'bathtub' combustion chamber, into which projects the sparking plug. A swirl-inducing ramped channel connects the two chambers, through which the mixture is pushed from the inlet valve zone to the main chamber by the piston on its compression stroke. This gives a low turbulence, concentrated charge round the sparking plug, which enables rapid and complete burning of very lean mixtures to take place under a very high compression ratio. Of course, in simple terms, the leaner the mixture and the higher the compression ratio, the more efficient the engine.

For the production May-headed V12, a 12.5:1 compression

was decided on, using a new high-power amplifier, twin-coil system to provide the 100% greater ignition energy required. As the mixture combustion now took place in the cylinder head, flat-topped pistons replaced the dished type, and the latest-type Lucas digital electronic fuel injection was reprogrammed to suit the new lean-burn characteristics of the engine, which was named the 'HE', standing for High Efficiency. With the announcement of the HE range on July 15, 1981, Jaguar were the first to get the May system into production. The results were well worth the effort – and the £½-million expense – of modifying the cylinder head plant at Radford to machine the new combustion chambers into the previously 'flat' heads.

While economy had been the main aim, extra efficiency meant extra power, too, and this prompted Jaguar to raise the final-drive ratio to 2.88:1, which took the top speed up to around 155mph. But more importantly, steady-speed fuel consumption improved dramatically – on the official urban cycle the HE gave (with previous figures in brackets) 15.6mpg (12.7), at 56mph 27.1 (21.9), and at 75mph 22.5 (18.6). In practice this made 20mpg a real proposition for an XJ-S, a figure of great pyschological importance!

Motor tested an XJ-S HE in October 1981 and confirmed the improvement – the latest car was 21% more economical at 16.3mpg overall than their previous road-test XJ-S, this figure including performance-testing. The journal also commented that 'it is now possible to achieve an astounding 22mpg at an average (over 650 miles) of more than 62mph' – which required driving the XJ-S at 80mph whenever possible.

It was a pity that these benefits were, to a certain extent, lost on cars sent to the United States. There, emission regulations enforced the continued use of catalytic converters, no less than eight being used on the Jaguar to reduce carbon monoxide, hydrocarbon and nitrogen oxides to carbon dioxide and nitrogen (by, in effect, burning). A Federal XJ-S would typically return as little as 10mpg during fast driving, and there was a fairly drastic performance penalty as well, 0-100mph taking around 21 seconds, as opposed to 17 for the European example. More expensive lead-free fuel had to be used as well, as lead additives 'poison' the platinum-rhodium crystals contained in the converters.

Both externally and inside the cockpit the car had changed, too, partly in response to customer feedback in the States, which clearly indicated that the XJ-S was regarded more as a luxury sports coupe than a sports car – which meant that the austere black plastic facia was not liked. The result was that at last the XJ-S was trimmed appropriately, with real leather replacing vinyl on the door casings, centre console and rear quarter trim panels, and – above all – hand-crafted wood veneer appeared on the facia, centre switch panel and door cappings. These improvements enriched the whole interior of the car.

The opportunity was also taken to adopt some Series 3 modernizations: there was a new leather-bound Series 3-type steering wheel, revised instrument and switch graphics, a delay wipe facility and revised wiper blade operation to clear a greater area of the screen, improved electric window switches, a timer-linked rear window heater element, a courtesy light delay (plus red guard lamps in the door pockets to provide a 'door open' warning), an improved central locking system to allow both doors to be locked by either of the exterior or interior locks on each door (the centre console door lock switch was deleted) and a new range of interior trim colours. In the boot, the spare wheel and battery box were now carpeted and a Series 3-type courtesy light fitted.

Outside, the HE was distinguished by new dome-type alloy wheels with a 6½-inch rim width and a jaguar head in the centre, Dunlop D7 tyres, a tapering, twin coachline along the length of the body, Series 3-type plated-top bumpers, US-style side repeater lights and black-finished scuttle-mounted heater/air-conditioner intakes and wiper arms. New badging appeared with the all-important 'HE' symbol appearing on the left-hand side of the bootlid, and a new antique-finish medallion embossed with the jaguar head (vaguely reminiscent of the original XK 120 badge) featuring on the bonnet.

Helped by the combination of better fuel economy, greater reliability and (in the United States) a 24-month/36,000-mile warranty, the XJ-S quickly became a best-seller at home and abroad. But Jaguar, and John Egan in particular, were intent on widening the car's appeal still further. The result was the XJ-S 3.6.

To Jaguar, the new car also represented the twin opportunities of trying out 'in service' the new AJ (Advanced Jaguar) 6 engine destined for the XJ-saloon replacement, and restyling the XJ-S to get rid of the infamous (?) flying buttresses and create an open Jaguar once more. The result was a lighter, sportier XJ-S with better economy and the huge advantage (to the enthusiast driver) of a five-speed manual gearbox.

Two models with the new engine were offered: the XJ-S 3.6, which retained the original XJ-S profile, and the XJ-SC 3.6 with its attention-getting cabriolet roof. A convertible XJ-S had been toyed with from early on in the model's career and even received a code name (XJ28 – the standard XJ-S had been XJ27), but lack of money or imagination, or the general depression which enveloped the XJ-S, prevented it becoming a serious proposition. When John Egan arrived at Jaguar, in 1980, everything changed and within months an open XJ-S was created. From this prototype was engineered a fully-productionized version, though the decision was taken to put some of the more specialized work out.

The necessary panelwork was thus placed with the Park Sheet Metal Company, at Exhall, near Coventry, and the tailoring and installation of the Targa-type hood with Aston Martin Tickford. The XJ-SC starts life as a standard XJ-S bodyshell at the Castle

Bromwich works, except for the omission of the roof and rear header panel; Park Sheet Metal then fit a new rear deck panel (having removed those buttresses!), strengthen the floorpan through additional stiffening of the transmission tunnel and a new crossmember, and install the centre crossbar – which incorporates one of the two tubular steel roll-over bars (the other is contained within the cant-rails over the door apertures), this one extending down to sill level.

The shell travels back to Castle Bromwich for painting, then on to Browns Lane for installation of mechanical components and trim. The usual checking and road-testing procedure follows, after which it's off to Bedworth to fit the hood and Targa panels. The completed car then returns to Jaguar, rejoins the XJ-S line and undergoes a final check and quality audit before being despatched to a dealer.

The open-top arrangements allow the driver quite a choice. They consist of two fabric-covered interlocking panels making up the detachable roof (placed in a storage envelope carried in the boot when not erected), a 'half-hardtop' made from double-skinned GRP and carrying a built-in heated rear window, and a

The AJ6 engine with its twin-overhead-camshaft, four-valves-per-cylinder head; note the long intake pipes and the tilt of the engine.

rear hood with its own window which can be erected instead of the hardtop. When lowered, the hood stows away below the rear deck-line, folded under a padded cover. Thus almost saloon-car comfort and silence can be enjoyed with the rigid panels in place, or semi-open-air sports car motoring with them removed and the rear hood down.

The new engine used in the latest XJ-S variants has been far more than just another engine option, of course – on it hangs the whole future of Jaguar, for it is scheduled to replace the revered XK engine in 1985 as Jaguar's mainstream power unit. Its use in the low-volume XJ-S was very much akin to Jaguar offering the first XK engine in the XK 120 and the V12 engine in the E-type prior to either of these being seen in the saloon cars for which they were originally intended – in all three cases a useful 'running-in' period was gained so that any minor problems on the engine build line, or in the power unit itself, could be sorted out before mainstream production began in earnest.

The 3,590cc, 91 × 92mm all-aluminium AJ6 engine emerged in its final form only after exploratory exercises centered around straight-six, V6 and V8 variations of the 12-cylinder engine, and around updated versions of the faithful XK engine. The former were abandoned because they were either insufficiently refined or of too small a capacity for a Jaguar, and the latter because too many of the dated features of the XK engine (like its weight, the crankcase split along the crankshaft centreline and the less than ideal studding arrangements for the cylinder head) would have been retained. So in the end a completely new block was decided upon and the previously intended use of all the existing V12 manufacturing plant abandoned (with the happy side-effect of allowing the fabulous V12 engine to continue in production after 1985, as its machinery would not, after all, be required to make the new power unit).

The new block, which continued well below the centreline of the seven-main-bearing crankshaft and used interference-fit dry liners, carried a cast-iron crankshaft which was easier to machine and generally cheaper to manufacture than Jaguar's traditional forged variety. It was surmounted by an up-to-the-minute four-valve-per-cylinder aluminium head, this arrangement of the valves giving excellent breathing and lower mechanical stresses. Jaguar stuck to chains for operating the twin overhead camshafts, just as they had done for the 12-

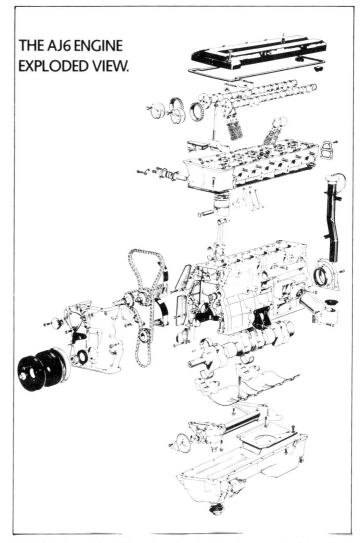

THE AJ6 ENGINE EXPLODED VIEW.

Exploded view of the AJ6 engine, showing how its new aluminium block extends below the crankshaft centreline; bucket tappets and chain drive systems are retained, however.

The XJ-S Eventer, by Lynx, must be about the quickest and most exclusive estate car in the world! A number have been built, and one was used by Penelope Keith in the popular TV series *To the Manor Born*.

cylinder engine, and also used basically the same, well-proven bucket tappet arrangements as in the old XK unit.

Naturally, fuel-injection was used (the Lucas/Bosch P digital type) and a 9.6:1 compression ratio was chosen; this gave 225bhp at 5,300rpm and 240lb/ft of torque at 4,000rpm, comparing very favourably with the fuel-injected 4.2 XK unit's 205bhp at 5,000rpm and 236lb/ft of torque at 3,750rpm – or the 5.3 engine's 299/318 figures, too, for that matter. Also, one of the XK engine's biggest disadvantages had been overcome – its weight. The new engine scaled 430lb, compared with 553lb for the XK, both in test-bed condition; the V12 weighed 640lb, incidentally.

The original XJ57 (the AJ6-engined XJ-S) was running by the spring of 1980, originally with what was termed the '2000' series block, a sand-cast open-deck unit with wet liners and of 3.8 litres; the '3000' series closed-deck block with its dry liners superceded it – a 3.8-litre version was in the running for a while until it was decided that the 3.6-litre engine provided all the power and torque necessary. But there remain options for the future in the forms of a 3.2-litre 'economy' version and larger-capacity 'performance' engine with a longer stroke.

Engineer Paul Walker admits that substituting the new 3.6-litre engine for the 5.3-litre V12 in the XJ-S represented a challenge if performance was to be maintained; the long inlet tracts are partly evidence of the need to get as much low and mid-range torque out of the engine as possible. Chassis changes to the car were few, just softer front springs (reduced from 423 to 329lb/in), a very slightly thinner anti-roll bar (by 1/16in to 0.811in – the XJ-S proved very sensitive to roll bar diameters) and the deletion of the rear anti-roll bar altogether. This would normally tend to increase understeer, but the right balance was obtained due to the reduction of weight over the front wheels courtesy of the AJ6 engine. Castor angle remained the same (it had been discreetly changed from 2.5 to 3.5 degrees about two years previously to crispen up response a little) but a slightly stiffer torsion bar was used in the power steering, giving a little more driver effort. The aim was to produce a slightly more positive, sporty feel to the car without interfering with the XJ-S's famed handling/ride balance; 'a more responsive car that turns in a little faster for the sporting driver', in Paul Walker's words.

The general feeling amongst those who tried the new variants was that Jaguar had succeeded in this, *Motor* commenting on the car's improved turn-in characteristics (even if the damping still allowed a certain amount of float over undulations taken at speed); *Autocar* also appreciated 'a welcome improvement in response'. Performance compared to the V12-engined car had really suffered very little – *Autocar* found their coupe reached a mean 141mph and, at 6.7 seconds, equalled the former's 0-60mph time. The time to 100mph was 19.7 seconds, 4 seconds down on the HE.

Much of the credit for this relatively small differential lies with the new car's transmission – the Getrag five-speeder. The use of a German-made gearbox might seem at variance with Jaguar tradition at first glance, but the factory had 'gone-out' for transmissions ever since they bought American Borg-Warner automatic gearboxes for the Mark VII saloon back in 1950, while the competition E-type of 1963 (though admittedly not a true production car) had used the German ZF five-speed manual box.

Together with the slightly tauter handling, the new gearbox made the XJ-S into much more of a real sports car. The driver could now select exactly the right ratio for any given road condition, and in particular the irksome refusal of the V12's

The same company, also noted for its D-type restorations, produced a true convertible XJ-S long before Jaguar's own cabriolet arrived.

The return of Jaguar to racing has resulted in a renewed interest in modified road Jaguars – this is TWR's spoilered and skirted version on duty as a course car at Donington (a works racing XJ-S is in the background, just before the start of the 1984 ETC round).

automatic gearbox to kick down into first at above 30mph was not encountered. This meant that on all but motorways the new 3.6 could cover the ground every bit as quickly as the 5.3 – and a good deal more economically, giving 17.6mpg under road-test conditions and 22-24mpg with gentler use.

Not that the AJ6 engine's installation was rated by everyone as a total success; both the British journals mentioned thought that the old XK unit could still teach the youngster a thing or two about smoothness, at least at mid-range or lower rpm, and the Getrag five-speed gearbox was found on occasion to be a little obstructive – an aspect not helped by a heavy clutch, which needed to be depressed fully to produce a baulk-free change. The overrun fuel cut-off contributed a little jerkiness when the Lucas fuel injection system re-introduced petrol at 800rpm as well, but this was soon to be cured by reprogramming the computer.

This little hiccup was really the legacy of a fairly late change of policy in the transmission department, as an advanced automatic gearbox (with optional manual selection built-in) as used on the latest BMWs was originally scheduled for the 3.6.

The Forward Engineering Company, of Birmingham, make this XJ-SS, adopting the name Lister-Jaguar as Brian Lister, who made the near-invincible Lister-Jaguar of the 1950s, has also been much involved in the project. Engine modifications, including an expansion of the capacity to 6.4 litres, are also offered.

However, the development required for this installation took longer than expected and so Jaguar opted for the simpler Getrag manual box; but the fuel injection computer had already been programmed for the automatic unit, hence the slightly jerky cut-in. The existing Jaguar/Rover '77mm' box wasn't used, incidentally, because it was already at its limit so far as engine torque was concerned.

The new models certainly emphasized the revival in the fortunes of the XJ-S, which had been evident from the moment the HE model had been introduced. Total XJ-S sales in 1980 had been 1,768; in 1983, the figure was 4,500! Anything up to 10,000 a year is envisaged for the late 1980s, though most of these will be coupes (either 5.3 or 3.6) as the new cabriolet is being built only to order and at a necessarily slower rate. It will, however, be offered in V12 form as well eventually.

Demand for the 3.6-litre cars was high and a waiting list soon developed; this was despite them being priced somewhat higher than some expected – £19,248 for the coupe and £20,756 for the cabriolet, the latter only £1,000 less than the XJ-S HE. Still, the majority of rivals remained dearer – the nearest equivalent Mercedes was now the 380SEC, which cost £29,930, the BMW 635CSi was £24,995, and the Porsche 928S Series 2 £30,679. Of the whole bunch, *Autocar* reckoned that despite its known shortcomings, the 3.6 Jaguar 'so clearly offers the best blend of qualities for the price; superb noise refinement and ride, with good handling, largely effortless performance, competitive levels of economy for the class, and air conditioning . . . it remains a hard act for the others to follow'.

Rather overshadowed by the launch of the dashing cabriolet and the exciting new engine, the XJ-S HE nevertheless continued as the ultimate high-performance Jaguar, and for 1984 several further refinements were added – improved stereo radio/cassette with digital tuning, a trip computer, cruise control and headlamp wash/wipe, all of which were extras on the smaller-engined cars. This made the car better value than ever; those used to forking out hundreds – or even thousands – of dollars or pounds for additional equipment on other prestige makes almost as a matter of course found the simple statement in Jaguar's XJ-S HE catalogue: 'Optional extras: none', particularly impressive . . .

Ironically, the very model which looked like becoming the first casualty in the XJ range has become one of the strongest sellers; still produced in relatively small quantities, the XJ-S does not contribute as much profit as the more numerous saloons, but the unit return is high and with its glamorous image (and recent international competition successes) it enhances the entire range. The irony is increased by the fact that the XJ-S is set to outlive the saloons from which it sprang by many years – yet proving, as it approaches the 1990s, how remarkable was the original 1968 XJ design. For it seems that the same basic chassis concept will still be providing some of the highest standards of ride, handling and comfort obtainable more than 20 years after it first entered production. Few other designs can, or ever will, be able to claim as much.

CHAPTER 7

The XJ in competition

From XJ12Cs to XJR-5s

The success which came to the team of XJ-S cars run by Tom Walkinshaw in the European Touring Car Championship is well-known, and in all probability represents the peak of the XJ series' limited but exciting – and sometimes controversial – competition career. The ETC victories have done much to offset the bad memories of the first official venture onto the race track by an XJ, which began back in 1976.

This, of course, was the brave try by another independent race engineer, Ralph Broad, who persuaded Derek Whittaker and Alex Park (who were then heading the troubled post-Stokes BL complex of companies) to let him prepare XJ12Cs for the European Touring Car Championship. Broad had longed for the chance to race the V12 Jaguar engine ever since it first appeared, and had unsuccessfully approached Jaguar with plans in that direction for the XJ-S (even before it had been announced) when Geoffrey Robinson was in office. He had better luck when he cut out Jaguar and went direct to the purse string holder, BL. From that moment, Jaguar had no control, and only a limited involvement in what then transpired.

BL were in dire need of an image-boost, and it seemed that doing well in a prestigeous international motor racing championship would fit the bill; Broad convinced them that the Jaguar was the tool with which to do it. The coupe was chosen because the XJ-S did not appear to quite conform to the FIA 'saloon' definition in respect of some interior dimensions, and could therefore have been challenged on that score by opposing teams. That particular championship ran under Appendix J Group 2 regulations, redrafted for 1976 and so giving the new Leyland-backed team (who were experienced in Group 2 racing

– Broad had long been successful with Minis, Escorts and, from 1974, BL's Triumph Dolomites) a slightly greater chance against their main protagonists, BMW, who had years of saloon-car racing experience behind them.

But the Southam-based concern did not receive their first coupe until September 1975, and while it appeared in its heavily modified Group 2 form in March 1976 for the benefit of the press, there was still a vast amount of development work left to make the heavy car raceworthy. A string of debut postponements followed as Broad fought for reliability, and the car was not be seen publicly until September – on home ground for the Tourist Trophy race at Silverstone. The mood of the crowd bordered on the ecstatic when Derek Bell put the 500bhp Jaguar on pole position and then led for virtually all of the first nine laps. But the car had already dropped well down the field due to tyre problems before it was finally put out by a broken drive-shaft while David Hobbs was driving.

A huge amount of development work was put in hand over the winter, and two new cars emerged in time for the first ETC round in March 1977 at Monza; but it was to be the beginning of a miserable season. No Jaguars finished at Monza because of oil starvation, caused by surge under heavy braking, a recurring problem that plagued the BMWs, too; at the Salzburgring, drive-shaft failure sidelined the British cars; the next two rounds were missed while further testing was carried out; then, on the Czechoslovakia circuit of Brno, Bell retired with a broken gearbox, though the Fitzpatrick/Schenken car limped to third place in its class, 16th overall, to record the XJC's first finish; at the all-important Nurburgring round, Fitzpatrick astonished

While Jaguar always denied a true works involvement, the appearance in 1976 of Ralph Broad's highly modified XJ12C was the nearest thing to an official Jaguar on European race tracks since 1956. The car above is the Group 2 racer testing in March, but it only appeared in one race, six months later at the Silverstone TT, when it failed to finish. Two new coupes appeared for 1977 in updated livery. The car pictured below is being driven at Silverstone by Tim Schenken. Immensely fast, their lack of reliability doomed any chance of success for these cars.

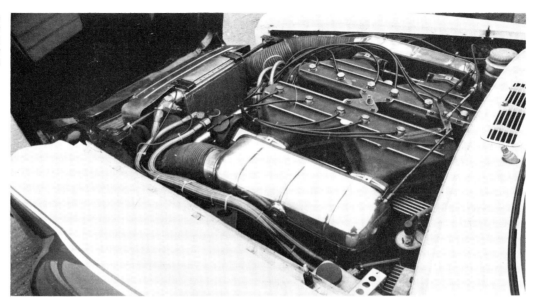

The engine bay of the 1977 XJ12C, the fuel-injection air ducts almost entirely masking the engine itself; note the oil cooler mounted behind the water radiator. Power output was around 550bhp!

everyone – including himself – by recording fastest lap from a rolling start, but the engine failed on the second lap, leaving Bell and Rouse to finish second to Nilsson's BMW (the Swedish driver's last victory); Zandvoort saw lowly finishing positions after, amongst other things, persistent scavenge pump breakages in the new dry-sump system (which the rules had been altered to allow).

At the Tourist Trophy, at Silverstone, the Jaguars nearly made it. Qualifying fastest, it seemed possible at one stage in the race that the coupes driven by Bell and Rouse could make up the deficit caused by the thirsty Jaguars' extra pit stop (two, against the BMWs' one), but rain brought the effort to nought; Zandvoort saw the big coupes' last race – neither finished – and then came BL's announcement that the project was over.

Ralph Broad attributed the bulk of the team's problems to the weight of the car; undoubtedly that was a big factor, for while development of the V12 engine ensured that the cars were nearly always fast enough, the 27cwt which had to be carried imposed great strains on the braking system and tyres. But also, the entry of the cars into the fray was surely premature, and the

consequent lack of development showed badly; nor was the Broadspeed team unaffected by British Leyland politics. Nevertheless, the efforts and commitment of the Broadspeed mechanics, the drivers, and Ralph Broad himself bordered on the heroic, and it should not be forgotten that the cars had led every single race they had run in and had secured at least one lap record. Broad remains convinced that, given another season, the cars would have started winning.

Meanwhile, somebody else had chosen the XJ-S to race and, helped by a more favourable set of regulations and valuable prior experience of racing the V12 Jaguar engine in the Series 3 E-type, quickly gained the success that so painfully had eluded Broadspeed. This was Bob Tullius' Group 44 team, based at Herndon, Virginia, in the United States, who were already veterans of many Sports Car Club Of America championships with Triumph and (up to 1976) Jaguar V12 E-types. The XJ-S seemed to be a natural successor to the now-obsolete E-type, and after winning its very first race (at Lime Rock, in September 1976), Tullius decided to contest the professional Trans-Am Championship with one in 1977.

Broadspeed retained much of Jaguar's polished wood facia; some said that if they'd used more standard Jaguar components elsewhere the cars would have lasted better – but who knows? A close-ratio four-speed gearbox was fitted (similar to that used in the XJ-S of the period), which was questionable under the existing Group 2 rules.

Apart from oil surge, braking required a major engineering effort; this is the four-pot caliper used up front on the 1977 car. Note the extra fresh air supply via the pipe on the right.

Again, the results were a contrast to the struggles with the XJ coupe in Europe, and Tullius ended the 1977 season as winner of the driver's championship in the Trans-Am Category 1. Heavily supported by British Leyland Motors Inc (and Quaker State Oil), Tullius was in close contact with the factory and he told me he was puzzled at the time why Ralph Broad had never once sought to take advantage of Group 44's comparatively vast experience of modifying the Jaguar engine.

Anyway, the American team continued its winning way and in 1978 did even better – Tullius once again secured the driver's championship, while Jaguar gained the manufacturer's championship ahead of determined General Motors (Corvette) and Porsche opposition, thanks to the entry of a second Group 44 XJ-S towards the end of the season, driven by Brian Fuerstenau. For 1979, Group 44 concentrated on racing a Triumph TR8 (a V8-engined TR7 not seen officially in Britain).

An idea of the performance returned by the Group 44 XJ-S is provided by the track test of the car carried out by *Road & Track* magazine in May 1977; a 700lb reduction in weight and around 476bhp helped the car to 60mph in 5 seconds and 100mph in

It was the American Group 44 team which produced a winner in 1976, debuting its XJ-S well before the Broadspeed coupe hit the track in anger. Fielded in a much lower key way in a possibly less competitive branch of the sport, the XJ-S (usually driven by Bob Tullius) quickly gained success against its American V8-powered opponents.

Meticulous, even clinical, is the way to describe Group 44's workshops; the author took this picture in 1976 while the XJ-S was being given a pre-race checkover.

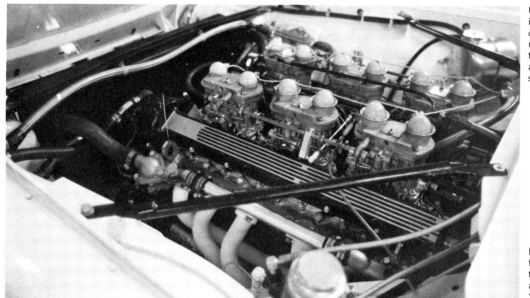

Unlike the British racing effort, Group 44 initially relied on six twin-choke Weber carburettors for their slightly less modified engine – taking advantage of their experience with the similarly aspirated V12 E-type they had raced with such success previously.

Following usual practice, the roll-over framework also contributed substantially to the Group 44 XJ-S's rigidity. No attempt has been made here to retain a 'Jaguar' interior!

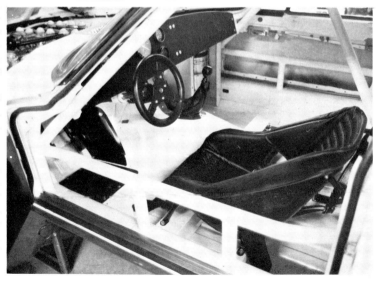

10.3 seconds, with an estimated top speed of 180mph with Daytona gearing. Interesting features included the maximum use of Jaguar components in the engine (only the Arias pistons, Crane camshafts and con-rod bolts came from outside sources), the two 'aircraft surplus' oil coolers, and the use of the roll-cage as a mounting for the semi-trailing links on the rear suspension. Tullius ascribed much of the car's success, not to an enormous power output, but to sheer handling, and the acceleration figures tend to bear this out – in a straight line the team's old E-type was probably as quick.

In Britain, Group 44's successes were inevitably not too well-known outside Jaguar enthusiast circles, even though Tullius secured the Trans-Am Championship as well as two driver's championships. But the entry of Tom Walkinshaw's two-car team in the European Touring Car Championship in 1982 was a different matter. Encouraged by four victories, including the Silverstone TT that year, the TWR team were given full official factory backing for 1983 – a courageous decision in a way by Jaguar after the debacle of the 5.3 coupes only a few years

A fresh team and a fresh start. Helped by new, favourable regulations, Tom Walkinshaw Racing quickly proved that the XJ-S could also be highly competitive on this side of the Atlantic. Here one of the two TWR cars circulates round Donington during the European Touring Car Championship race of 1982.

before, though – as they were quick to point out – the earlier attempt on the ETC was never an official Jaguar one, being a purely British Leyland project. Jaguar's pre-season publicity, in fact, pointedly ignored the Broadspeed effort and harked back instead to the very first European Touring Car Championship in 1963 – won by Peter Lindner's 3.8 Mark 2 Jaguar saloon.

Happily, Walkinshaw delivered the goods; the 1983 season saw him finish second in the driver's championship, with the XJ-Ss gaining five overall victories, while in 1984, the Jaguars showed almost complete domination of the series, finishing one-two-three on a number of occasions. BMW, which had reigned supreme since the early 1970s, at least had to concede defeat and rarely could any of the seemingly dozens of 635CSi coupes hold off the three green-and-white Jaguars. The British car's finest achievement was victory in the Spa-Francorchamps race in July – the first 24-hour race win for Jaguar since 1957 at Le Mans, which set the seal on Jaguar's official return to the race tracks of Europe. Walkinshaw himself won the driver's championship, and the team then set about preparing for the 1985 season.

The entry of the British XJ-Ss in the ETC was brought about by two main factors. Firstly, for 1982 the 12-round championship was to be run under new Group A regulations for four-seater touring cars, which ensured that they would be much nearer showroom specification than when the V12 coupes were racing, particularly in respect of engine modifications and bodywork (which had to be standard). The XJ-S's suspension – basically double-wishbone front and rear – was ideal for race-development within the regulations and, together with generous wheelarch clearances, enabled the maximum allowable rim and tyre widths to be used.

As for the engine, initial testing was carried out using Weber carburettors, but fuel injection was employed when the cars began racing; standard crankshaft and cylinder blocks were used, and power was kept to around 400bhp initially to ensure maximum reliability – all ETC rounds being endurance events of 3 to 4 hours duration, another factor traditionally in favour of the Jaguar. During 1982, the cars competed against the elderly but still very fast 3.0 CSL BMWs of basically the same type that had vanquished the V12 coupes in 1976 and 1977, though from 1983, the aforementioned 635 CSi coupes took up the torch for

Official rather than overt backing for TWR came from Jaguar in 1983; here is Tom Walkinshaw with one of the latest cars (of the two raced, one was all-new, the other an updated 1982 car), on the announcement of the programme.

The strictly functional interior of the 1983 TWR XJ-S (below left) with a rev-counter taking pride of place in front of the driver. Below, the surprisingly standard-looking engine bay. The regulations limited modifications and standard-type fuel injection was used; but higher-compression pistons, new cam profiles and other changes increased the power from 299 to around 375bhp. Alan Scott is TWR's Jaguar engine specialist.

BMW, while the surprisingly fast Volvo Turbos ran in the top three on occasions. Ralph Broad may have said that 'his' coupes were beaten by weight, but due to the regulations the TWR Jaguars, at 1,400kg, actually weighed more, and yet Walkinshaw coped; but due to the same regulations, the XJ-Ss were some 100bhp down on power, which must have helped the brakes at least.

While very definitely not a saloon, the sports-racing, American-built XJR-5 should be mentioned, as of course it was powered by the same V12 engine as used in the XJ-S and XJ12 models. Again the product of Group 44's enterprise, the XJR-5 made history by being the first Jaguar-powered car to run at Le Mans since 1964; designed by top American racing car designer Lee Dykstra for endurance racing, its engine was bored out to 6 litres and mated to a Hewland five-speed gearbox, though unlike many of its contemporaries it remained normally aspirated. Brake horsepower was something in the region of 600, and some 1½ seasons of highly competitive North American IMSA Camel GT racing were completed before Jaguar made the decision to enter the cars at Le Mans.

Rear suspension of the 1983 XJ-S, TWR-style. An entirely new lower wishbone was used, and the discs placed outboard. Certain aspects of this suspension will be seen on XJ40. While a normal jack steadies the car centrally, the built-in air jack (left) is actually supporting it.

A major component in TWR's success has been the ability of the pit crew and mechanics; pit-stops for fuel (this is during the very wet Donington ETC round in 1983) and minor attention are usually models of efficiency and speed.

Another new colour scheme arrived for 1984, this time the XJ-S ETC contenders being painted largely in British Racing Green. Here Win Percy tests the number 2 car at Silverstone in March.

Ahead of the opposition, and virtually in the finishing order at Brno, Czechoslovakia, in June, when the XJ-Ss took first, second and third places! The BMW 635CSi coupes were increasingly looking slow and old-fashioned, and were even being hounded by the turbocharged Volvos.

The greatest victory for the TWR Motul Jaguars in 1984 was in the 24-hour Spa-Francorchamps race in July, hailed by John Egan as the most significant win by a Jaguar in Europe since the marque's last Le Mans success in 1957. Here the Walkinshaw/Heyer/Percy XJ-S surges to a three-lap victory ahead of the Schintzer BMW.

This dealer-entered XJ5.3 ran in the saloon car race which accompanied the 1979 South African GP, but it failed to produce a significant result; an unusual effort, though!

In Britain, the Jaguar Driver's Club usually lays on races for standard production Jaguars and both XJ saloons and XJ-Ss take part – this is a Silverstone dice between the XJ5.3Cs of Peter Curtis (left) and Derek Pearce.

This chapter would not be complete without a picture of the XJR-5, Group 44's endurance racing car powered by the Jaguar V12 engine. Just as basically the same XK engine powered Jaguar road cars and Le Mans winners in the 1950s, so may the V12 engine prove capable of doing so in the 1980s!

This move was indicative of the second reason behind the appearance of 'official' Jaguars in international racing from 1982 – the desire by the new management under John Egan to broadcast the fact that Jaguar were alive, well and kicking, and that an aggressive sales campaign was underway, backed by vastly improved product quality. While neither of the two XJR-5s finished the 1984 Le Mans race, they certainly didn't disgrace themselves, having run in the top three on occasion before being eliminated by relatively small problems; their performance, together with the domination of the TWR XJ-Ss in the European Touring Car Championship, certainly had the desired impact on the market. For a manufacturer, racing is all about creating an image and demonstrating speed and reliability. The XJ-S, above all, succeeded in this, and it helped to re-establish Jaguar as a manufacturer of truly sporting cars in a manner which had not been seen since the days of the well-loved Mark 2 saloon and E-type in the mid-1960s.

CHAPTER 8

Buying an XJ Jaguar

The choice, the inspection and the test

Compared to an 'ordinary' family saloon, a new or nearly new Jaguar XJ is expensive; but as with most big-engined, luxury cars with a substantial thirst for petrol, time is a great leveller, and after 10 years or so, most four-door XJs fetch little more than something nice and cheap to run, like a Ford Escort. This makes an old XJ appear a tempting proposition, but while there are ways round it – which we'll discuss further on – the eager prospective buyer should always remember that he or she is also committed to the maintenance costs of a £15,000 vehicle, not that of an Escort . . .

For most of us, the money available governs the age, or to a slightly lesser extent, the condition of an XJ we can hope to buy; and so far as the initial purchase price goes, almost anyone can afford a running, 'MoT'd XJ because they begin (in Great Britain at least) at or even slightly below the £300 mark. Your expenditure subsequently is, to some extent, a matter of luck, as even by paying 10 times that amount you will not be able to guarantee against major failures, simply because a £3,000 car will still be quite old and could have covered an extensive mileage. Obviously, though, there are ways to minimize the risk of a bad buy.

First, a quick review of the *types* of XJ available. As a broad rule, and providing the car is in good shape, the performance, ride, handling and even general refinement are much the same, whether you are buying a 1968 car or a one-year old example, so good was the original XJ6. About the only exceptions here are the fuel-injected versions of the 4.2 and 5.3-litre cars, which are noticeably faster (and a little less thirsty) than their carburettor-equipped predecessors. So the updates which came with each

new series were - as we have seen – concerned more with ergonomics and cosmetics than with fundamental engineering changes.

For sheer convenience, the Series 3 is the better car; the heating/ventilation is more effective, there is a wiper delayed action, lumbar support for the seats, and so on. Likewise, Series 2 cars score over Series 1s (so named only after the introduction of the newer model, of course) by virtue of their modern stalk controls, better heater, and instruments all in front of the driver. But there again, Series 1 enthusiasts love their cars for the very reason that the minor instruments are centrally placed *à la* Mark 2 and E-type Jaguars, and for the aesthetically pleasing row of sturdy, black switches on the central console. As for exterior looks, that is even more a matter of personal taste!

At the time of writing – mid-1984 – no XJ had reached a collector's status to the extent that it was markedly appreciating in value. Even the two-door coupe, labelled 'classic' even during its own production lifetime, was still by and large dropping in value, or at best just holding it. However, Series 1s have certainly bottomed-out and will never be cheaper, and the same applies to early Series 2s, which means that if you were to buy a really splendid Series 1 (a rarity in itself) and kept it in that condition, you would be likely to at least see your money back on selling it in a few years' time. Of the early cars, the short-wheelbase XJ12 is probably the best bet in this respect on account of its rarity; a mere 720 right-hand drive examples were built, and surely only a few hundred now remain in Britain.

Now for how to assess the condition of the car you're thinking of buying. The first stage is a preliminary walk round it, looking

for regular door gaps, the condition of the chrome, and whether there are any ripples or dents in the bodywork. Rust holes on the outer panels will be obvious (though use a small magnet to detect filler) but examination of three or four areas should quickly decide whether the car is a good prospect or not. These are the radius arm mountings on the rear suspension, the inner wings inside the engine compartment adjacent to the battery tray and above the radiator expansion tank, the front crossmember under the radiator, and the roof above the rear window. If any or all of these places display rot, then unless you are fairly well versed in body-welding techniques the car may be beyond economic repair.

Other typical XJ rust points are shown in the pictures; if you find a car with very few of them, be suspicious – the chances are that the rust has been covered up by oversills or filler, and the aforementioned magnet is useful. The exception is the Series 3 range, which has markedly more durable bodywork, thanks to the long-overdue introduction of wax injection into body cavities which began with this model. The XJ-S bodyshell must be checked for rot in the front footwells (the air conditioner drainpipe can become blocked, causing water to leak into the floor) and in the bootwell, where heat from the exhaust can cause condensation.

For a mechanical assessment of, firstly, the straight-six cars, try to begin with the engine 'cold' – some mechanical noises will be at their worst before the oil has warmed up. But before turning the key, take a look at the water in the radiator and the oil on the dipstick; if there are signs that the two are mixing, it usually means a failed cylinder-head gasket. Then start the engine and, with the bonnet open, listen for timing chain noise (the lower one is the more difficult to replace) and general clatter from the cylinder head. While the odd noisy tappet is no real problem, excessive noise could indicate wear in the tappet buckets and sleeves, which is expensive to eradicate.

In the engine bay, feel along the chassis members, especially under the battery and radiator header tank. Serious corrosion here means that extensive repairs will be necessary.

Also examine the crossmember in front of the radiator, looking down between this and the grille. Normally it will not be exposed like this, unless the bumper has been removed.

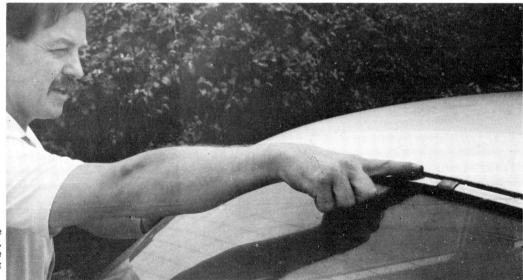

Another indication of a bad car could be rot in the roof, just above the rear screen, also indicated by staining on the headlining inside. Water tends to collect under the rubber seal.

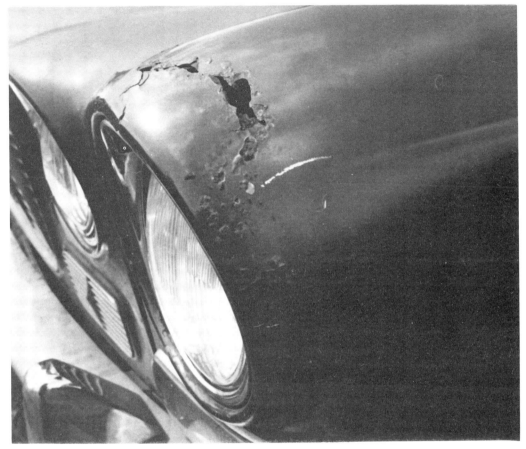

Rust in exterior panels is easier to spot; while later XJs had mud shields, earlier ones suffered from mud thrown up into the headlight peaks, which consequently rotted.

There are some useful checks you can do before moving off. With the engine running, rock the steering wheel to feel if the power steering is working correctly, then pump the brake pedal; the engine note should drop slightly, indicating the vacuum assistance is basically functioning. Then keep the brakes on and move the selector on an automatic car from D to R a few times, listening for 'clunks' as the drive is taken up by the rear end. This will also tell you if the transmission 'bites' properly as drive is engaged.

Finally, before you move off it will pay to check the tyre pressures; if they're uneven or too soft it will influence handling and braking and may cause you to draw wrong conclusions. While you're in the vicinity, check the condition of the tyres and watch especially for wear on the inside of the tread; this could mean worn suspension, with wear in top ball-joints and inner wishbone mountings at the front giving excess negative camber.

On the road, get the oil and water up to operating temperature, ensuring that the oil gauge reads 40psi at

119

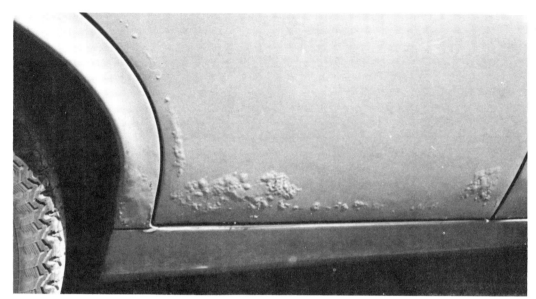

Doors rot where the skin meets the door frame; this picture also shows incipient rust in the rear wing adjacent to the sill.

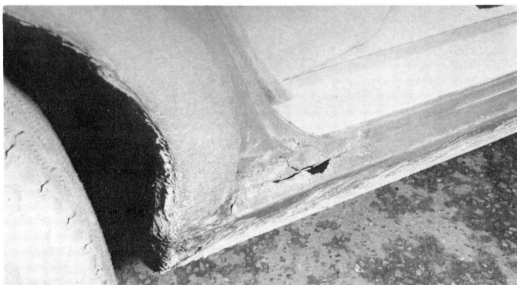

If you open the door, holes in the top of the sill and 'B' post might well be disclosed.

Rusting of the rear valance and side panels (the left-hand one has been removed from this car along with the petrol tank) is very common, but these items are relatively easily replaced.

Another common rust spot is round the rear wheelarch (below), where water collects between the outer and inner wings; this is an extreme example, and it shows that the centre wall of the sill has rotted away above the radius arm mounting. If possible, remove the spare wheel (below right) and examine all round the well, including the far end.

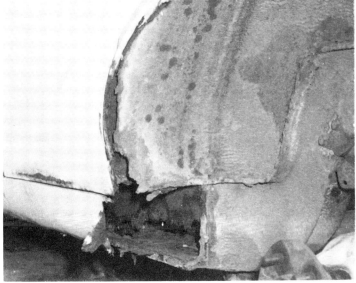

The boot area also rusts along the seam just below the fuel pumps (foreground) and the box section along the opening (top centre).

One check for accident damage resulting in a displaced front subframe (below left) is to roughly measure the distance between the rear of the tyre and the wing with your fingers – then go round the other side and see if that gap is the same. Then check for uneven tyre wear – a worn inside shoulder like this (below) on a front tyre could mean incorrect suspension geometry caused by worn top ball-joints and wishbone mountings.

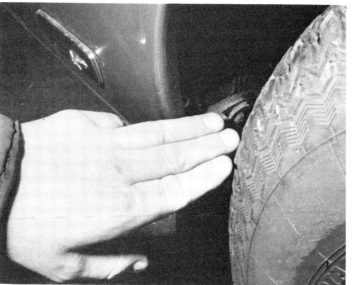

A typical Series 1 engine bay; checks here include looking for excessive oil leakage, bad head and timing chain noise, making sure the Torquatrol fan hasn't seized, and whether engine numbers correspond to the car identification plate numbers.

The 4.2 block had a fairly thin cast-iron water jacket and this can crack if not frost-protected; if so, this is the area likely to suffer. Not to be confused with the propensity of the block to crack between the cylinders, visible only on lifting the head.

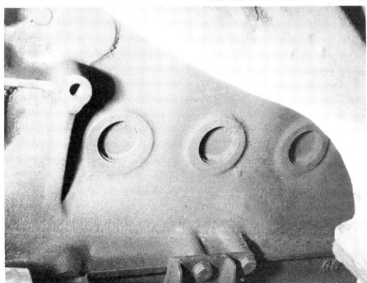

3,000rpm and above. Accelerate, watching for quite prompt and smooth changes from the automatic gearbox, and for any sign of throttle steer; this, plus clonks from the rear end, means rear suspension wear. Float or wallow indicates worn-out dampers – and remember you may have six to replace! Higher-speed vibrations (over 70mph) are usually signs of an out-of-balance propeller shaft or worn UJs in the rear suspension. Braking should be powerful and free from pull, and a wobble from the brake pedal means the front discs have distorted and need replacing.

Manual XJs are fairly rare; checks on these include making sure the clutch shows no signs of slip (especially in top from about 35mph), that the gear lever moves quite easily, and that the synchromesh works effectively, including first. Listen for excessive noise in first and reverse gears, and try the overdrive which will probably be fitted – it should engage and disengage promptly.

Then, whatever the weather, try the heater, or the air conditioning if fitted. The XJ is practically built around these and replacing major units involves many hours of work; one

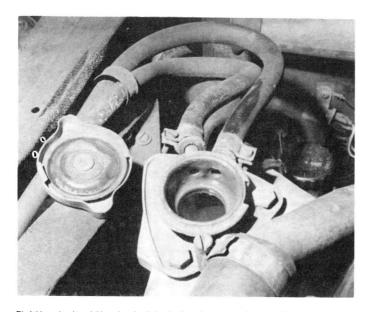

Fluid levels should be checked, including for contamination (this is the power steering reservoir). Also try to look at the automatic gearbox fluid – if it is a murky black, the bands have probably worn and the box may not have long to go.

could almost say of a used XJ, don't buy it if the heater leaks or doesn't function. It may quite well be something simple like a failed valve – but it might not!

Having come in from your drive, keep the engine running and let it idle for a minute or so – then blip the throttle and watch for blue smoke, which could mean bore wear. Next, switch off, open the bonnet and, with the aid of a rag, remove the oil filler cap – excessive fumes could indicate wear or a blown cylinder head gasket, the latter in turn making it highly probable that the cylinder block is cracked on its top face, quite a common fault on 4.2 engines.

Most of these tests can be applied to the V12 engine, which is just as durable as the XK unit – more so, if anything. However, being all-aluminium, it is more susceptible to ill treatment, and in particular to overheating caused by a hose leaking, or simple neglect on the part of the owner in keeping the radiator topped-

up. The most usual result is a failed head gasket, and you could begin by asking the owner if the car tends to use water, and by checking the coolant level – if it's down, be suspicious, particularly as a blown head gasket often results in the cylinder heads 'welding' themselves to the block, making removal very difficult. The correct mixture of anti-freeze is essential for the same reason, and again, if the radiator doesn't look as if it contains the right dilution, the engine probably hasn't been looked after.

Under the bonnet, with the engine running, try listening for bearing rumble (a correct 60 to 80psi 'hot' oil pressure reading doesn't necessarily mean that all the bearings are OK), timing chain noise, smoke from the exhaust, of course, when the engine is blipped after a period on idle and, under the car, oil leaks from the bellhousing area, which could mean a faulty rear main bearing seal – to replace that means removing the engine.

Both six and 12-cylinder cars share the same suspension, and in addition to the 'on the road' checks mentioned, look underneath for excessive oil leakage from the differential unit (which could mean an oil seal has gone, perhaps 'cooked' by the inboard rear brakes), and take note of the condition of the discs. Also check on the road whether the handbrake is effective (try applying it at around 30mph). Many repair jobs on the rear suspension and brakes mean dropping the rear subframe, which is not particularly difficult, but is a nuisance when all you want to do is replace a brake caliper, for instance.

If you intend to invest time and money on the XJ you buy, the condition of the interior is crucial if the effort is not to be partially or totally wasted, as an XJ with worn-out upholstery and splits in the door trim panels will never be an 'A1' car. Retrimming is prohibitively expensive, so examine the leather, in particular for tears and wear. Stained headlinings are a big minus point, too.

As for where to find your XJ, the classified columns in weekly motoring magazines mainly feature Series 3 cars now; for Series 1 and 2 XJs, look in the local paper, *Exchange & Mart*, and possibly *Motor Sport*. Or join the Jaguar Driver's Club, as their *Jaguar Driver* magazine has upwards of a dozen advertised each month. Series 1s, in any case, are getting slightly less common (especially good ones) and Series 2s are currently the most plentiful on the secondhand market.

The XJ's rear suspension is an exemplary design, but as it contains many moving parts it is expensive to repair. Besides the checks mentioned in the text, watch for separation of the rubber mountings.

The front suspension employs top and bottom ball-joints, which can wear, while the inner mountings for the wishbones can also deteriorate. On this car (due for restoration), the anti-roll bar has been disconnected.

If you want to regard your XJ as a long-term prospect, the interior condition is important. This is a quite well preserved Series 1 – its centre instrument panel was often hated by motoring writers of the time, but is now beloved by many enthusiasts; it hinges down in a few seconds for maintenance, by the way.

It is difficult to single out a 'best buy' – it depends to some extent on whether you want a hobby car which won't be accumulating a high annual mileage, or more of a working car for use every day. If you're in the former category, then an XJ12 of some description could be worth considering, as the extra petrol used compared with an XK-engined model will not be very significant over a small mileage – and because few people want them, they are incredibly good value for money. A 2.8-litre, with its known propensity for holing pistons, is similarly unloved and even cheaper, but frankly it represents a risk; you could be lucky and never have a moment's trouble, or you could hole a piston the first time you drive it.

The best car to put money into if you are looking for a long-term project is the coupe, especially, perhaps, the 5.3 car – after all, a mere 604 right-hand-drive Jaguar examples were built, a tiny quantity for a production car. However, long-term is the applicable phrase, and it's probable that true appreciation (taking into account inflation) from 1984-85 values will not occur until maybe four or five years have elapsed.

Older versions of the XJ-S are available for around the same prices as the coupes, but particularly as that car looks set for another five years of production, it is anybody's guess as to how pre-HE cars will fare pricewise. Perhaps a low-mileage manual example would be the one to choose – these will certainly be very rare in a few years' time. However, this is all sheer speculation, and really you should simply enjoy whatever XJ you've been able to buy, and forget about making money from it as a long-term investment!

CHAPTER 9

XJ spares and maintenance

Sources, clubs and specialists

As indicated in the previous chapter, an XJ or XJ-S is not a cheap car to run. It is quite possible that, technically, an earlier example may need several thousand pounds spent on it to bring it to anywhere near top condition if you employ expensive garage labour and buy all the parts new; for a car that has been bought for, say, £500, that is plainly uneconomic. Certainly, if you have a two or three-year-old Series 3 or XJ-S HE, by all means have it serviced at a main dealer – not that much should need doing and, if you've afforded that price of car in the first place, you can afford a main agent's labour charges!

So this chapter is really for the less pecunious, and the good news is that it is perfectly feasible to run an XJ on a very small budget – indeed, it needn't cost much more than, say, a Ford Granada or MGB to maintain. The secret is to buy the best car you can to start with, and then, if major units fail, replace them with secondhand ones. Of course, the precondition is that you should be able to do much of the work yourself, but even if you need paid assistance, by replacing whole units rather than having the original ones stripped down, repaired and rebuilt again, that can also be contained.

The logic of this is self-evident. Supposing a head gasket goes on your XJ6, you take the head off and find that the block is cracked – and you can also see that there's a lot of wear in the head, with the valves not looking too happy. Additionally, you know that if the bottom end of the engine is stripped, the chances are the crankshaft will be pretty worn, and you can feel quite a ridge in the bores. You have three alternatives: purchase an exchange rebuilt engine from a reputable specialist (cost: £900-£1,300 – and if it's much cheaper it probably has not been done properly), order all the new parts and rebuild the engine yourself (cost: £500-£800), or look around for a secondhand engine (cost: £100-£300 'heard running').

Yes, there's a risk with the third option and it's not ideal, but lots of people with old XJs don't have any alternative. Likewise, a worn-out rear suspension will cost upwards of £700 to rebuild, but a secondhand one, conveniently self-contained in its subframe, can probably be bought for £50-£200.

You can't, of course, take short cuts in 'safety' areas like brakes, steering and individual suspension components. But you can probably save money by shopping around – many parts firms, even BL and Jaguar themselves, have 'special offer' lines from time to time, and advantage can be taken of these; it can even be worth buying, say, a new brake caliper and putting it away even if you don't need it immediately, if the price is right. Jaguar Driver's Club events often include Jaguar autojumbles, and bargains can certainly be had there; 'spares for sale' feature prominently in the *Jaguar Driver*, too (only available to members, of course). A list of firms specializing in Jaguar parts can be found at the end of this chapter.

As we have seen, the XJ bodyshell leaves plenty of scope for the rust-bug, and most cars will need metalwork repairs at some stage. Much of this can tackled by the reasonably skilled do-it-yourselfer, though the more complex underbody work (like around the radius arm mountings) can be farmed-out to a competent body shop. A wide range of exterior body panels is available at reasonable prices, though original factory front wings are in the three-figure bracket. But if you're prepared to look, 'old stock' factory panels can often be found to aid your

Improving or restoring an XJ is not impossibly expensive if tackled in the right way. This car is being fitted with outer sills, a rear wheelarch section and a rear valance, work all within the scope of a competent DIY person.

This repair panel (below left) costs only a few pounds and will cover all the damage visible here; but note that the join with the inner wing must be made good as the panels are structural at this point. While rear-end repairs are being made and the petrol tanks removed (below), it is a good idea to replace the fuel line, which collects dirt and rots (you can buy everlasting copper replacements).

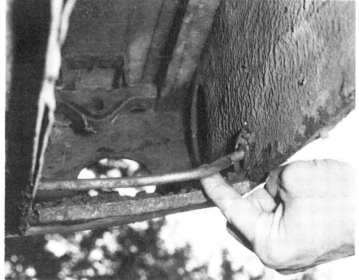

A full engine or cylinder head overhaul is expensive if done properly, but secondhand items can be considered. A home rebuild is feasible for the able amateur mechanic, however.

rebuild and your wallet.

In tracking down both new and used parts at the right price you'll find membership of the Jaguar Driver's Club very useful – write to the JDC at Jaguar House, 18 Stuart St, Luton, Bedfordshire (tel: 0582 419332) for a brochure and application form. There is an XJ Register within the club to help the interchange of XJ news and technical information, and by going along to your local JDC Area Centre (there are some 40 spread over Britain) you should quickly get to know local spares sources and be able to swop information and parts with fellow owners. Overseas, there are Jaguar clubs in most countries, and a letter to the JDC or to Special Facilities Dept, Jaguar Cars Ltd, Browns Lane, Allesley, Coventry, should elicit the address of the Jaguar club in your country.

Owning an older XJ is not necessarily a recipe for the easy life – there are cheaper and simpler cars to maintain – but the reward is a combination of ride, performance, handling, comfort and prestige that few other affordable cars can match. The XJ series will soon be out of production – perhaps it already is by the time you read this – and while its successor carries many advances with it, I'm sure that many XJ enthusiasts will maintain that their cars are special and represent a magnificent chapter in Jaguar's history.

Modifying the XJ range

A few years ago, only a minority of even the most hardened enthusiasts contemplated performance modifications for their current-model Jaguars; now that Jaguar have re-entered racing with the XJ-S and the XJR-5, the *marque* is re-acquiring its sporting image and, consequently, a number of people are keenly interested in making their XJ saloon or XJ-S look and go faster.

There are several firms specializing in this sort of work, including TWR, Forward Engineering and Jochen Arden in Germany; all three offer body spoiler kits, engine, gearbox and suspension modifications, though the prices are such that it is mostly the new-car owner who will be able to afford them. It is possible to order an enlarged V12 engine of either 5.7 or 6.4 litres from Forward Engineering, but the latter costs nearly £8,000 – cheap by comparison with the expense of modifying a Ferrari V12, but not affordable by everyone! Both Forward and TWR offer more efficient exhaust systems, larger brakes and – what, significantly, TWR rate as about the most important 'mod' of all – a five-speed manual gearbox.

Personalizing your XJ has become more popular in recent years; the addition of spoilers can make the car look very sporting.

Descending from these rather giddy realms, the more impecunious owner, if not satisfied with the performance of their standard XJ, can 're-align' their car towards handling and speed rather than ride and silence – in compromising between these factors you won't be able to beat Jaguar, so a small loss in refinement can be expected if an alteration to the standard specification is made.

Perhaps the easiest and cheapest way of improving the handling response of an XJ is to fit an inch smaller diameter steering wheel; this adds slightly to steering 'weight' and psychologically, at least, sharpens the response of the car and makes it feel even more precise at speed. The next step in this direction is to fit Koni, Spax or Bilstein adjustable dampers, set just a little harder than the original-equipment units. This, too, will tauten the car, eradicating any traces of wallow or transitional roll through an 'S' bend. Continuing this theme would be the fitment of Pirelli P7, Goodyear NCT or similar high-performance, low-profile tyres, but this is where the expense starts to creep in!

The dedicated enthusiast will want to use a manual-gearbox XJ as the basis for any modifications; amongst the Series 1 or 2 cars these are quite easily found, but are slightly less common amongst the Series 3s. A change from automatic to manual is possible, but not really economic unless you are prepared to do the work yourself. The same applies in converting a V12-engined saloon to manual, except that the correct four-speed gearbox is now hard to find. You might be better off looking for a manual-gearbox XJ-S – they're few and far between, but no more expensive than an automatic version when found.

So far as engines are concerned, it is relatively easy to get tuning parts for the six-cylinder XK engines, and bringing a Series 2 engine up to or exceeding the power output of a Series 3 injected unit is not difficult – a gas-flowed cylinder head with larger (1⅞in) inlet valves, plus either triple SUs or three Weber carburettors, will do the job nicely. The more experienced owner could do much of the work involved himself.

Modifying the V12 is not so easy, particularly with the fuel-injection engines, where the computer would need reprogramming if any changes were to be made. The most cost-effective method of raising the bhp of any Jaguar V12 engine is

A smaller-diameter steering wheel with a thicker rim helps promote steering feel and is relatively inexpensive. The manual XJ-S (above), the prototype Lister-Jaguar XJ-SS, has also been equipped with supplementary instruments. Harder dampers assist handling, while Forward Engineering market this bracket (above right), which bolts underneath the rear subframe to prevent tramp during fast take-offs from rest.

Twin-choke Weber carburettors have been used on the XK engine for extra power (30-40bhp more on average) since the early 1950s. This is a Series 1 car fitted with a big-valve head, a comparatively rare modification.

to fit a straight-through exhaust system, which can be as simple as making up new tailpipes omitting all but the front silencer boxes. This alone is worth from 15 to 30bhp. A similar increase would come from fitting Weber downdraught carburettors to a pre-fuel injection engine, but of course, unless you can find them secondhand, this is an expensive conversion.

As intimated previously, 2.8-litre Jaguars are not exactly hot sellers on the secondhand market, and very good examples can be picked up for a few hundred pounds; for the enthusiast prepared to put the work in, therefore, finding a bodily good 2.8 and swopping its engine for a 4.2 unit from, say, a crashed example is a good way to end up with a worthwhile XJ6. The cooling system, clutch linkages and the final-drive ratio are also affected by such a change, though. In the United States, the fitting of home-built V8s to older XJ12s has become a relatively common exercise, incidentally – unlike in the UK, secondhand engines (or even new ones) are not readily available.

One must add, however, that for most people an XJ Jaguar has ample performance, and unless you are very keen, your time and money are probably better spent in making sure that all the

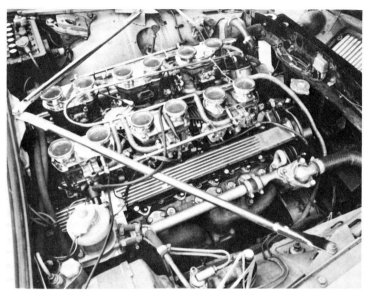

This impressive sight is of an early XJ12 fitted with no less than six downdraught Weber carburettors. Performance was considerably enhanced, but fuel consumption at around 13mpg was much the same as with the original Zenith-Strombergs.

More recently, tuners have modified the fuel injection system rather than used carburettors, as on this Forward Engineering XJ-S. Special modular economy kits are also offered, which cut out six cylinders on low throttle openings – Roger Bywater is the main exponent of these.

A very unusual engine bay – Ken Wadham has modified his XJ12 to run on the very simple but effective Fish carburettors, six in all. Much improved performance and economy is claimed.

standard parts on the car are working as the maker intended. This alone usually brings about a remarkable increase in performance, handling and braking behaviour in an older car of any description!

Firms supplying parts and services for XJs
In addition to the names included alpnabetically here, your local official Jaguar dealer should be able to obtain most mechanical parts, and 'factory' body and chrome items for later cars. For older cars, body repair panels and 'maintenance' parts, like oil filters, brake components, etc, can often be obtained from local accessory shops and motor factors – but, particularly with brake/suspension/steering parts, *only use recognized brands*. Note: The inclusion in this list of a company doesn't necessarily imply a recommendation by the author or publisher.

J.W. Bailey, 50 Latimer Gardens, Pinner, Middlesex.
Tel: 01-868 3441.
Brake parts specialist.

British Sports Car Centre, 299-309 Goldhawk Road, London W12.
Tel: 01-748 7823/4 or (Midlands branch) 0902 344916.
Body and mechanical parts, also servicing/repairs.

Burlen Services, Greencroft Street, Salisbury, Wilts.
Tel: 0722 21777.
Carburettor parts, new and exchange units.

FB Components, 35-41 Edgeway Road, Marston, Oxford.
Tel: 0865 724646/7.
Mail order specialists, parts, including export.

Forward Engineering Company, 780 Kingsbury Rd, Erdington, Birmingham B24 9PS.
Tel: 021-384 6000/6001.
Engine rebuilds and parts; 3.8, 4.2 and 5.3-litre road/race modifications; servicing; builders of Lister XJ-S.

Duncan Hamilton & Company, The Square, Bagshot, Surrey.
Tel: 0276 71010.
British agents for Arden body, chassis and engine tuning parts.

Barry Hankinson, Claypitts House, Buck Birch, Hereford.
Tel: 0989 65789.
Retrim materials, upholstery kits, etc.

Olaf P. Lund & Son, 40 Upper Dean St, Birmingham.
Tel: 021-622 1384.
New and reconditioned spares.

Lynx Engineering, 8 Castleham Road, St Leonards on Sea, Sussex.
Tel: 0424 51277.
Convertible XJ coupe and XJ-S, Eventer estate XJ-S, performance conversions.

G.H. Nolan, 1 St Georges Way, London SE15.
Tel: 01-701 2785.
All parts, body and mechanical.

Norman Motors, 100 Mill Lane, London NW6.
Tel: 01-431 0940.
Body and mechanical parts, mail order specialists, including export. Large stocks of secondhand items.

Phillips Garage, 206 Bradford St, Deritend, Birmingham B12 0RG.
Tel: 021-722 2000.
Reconditioned engines, engine parts, service and repairs.

Tom Walkinshaw Racing (TWR), 1 Station Field Industrial Estate, Kidlington, Oxford.
Tel: 08675 71565.
Body/engine/chassis conversions; maker of TWR XJ-S.

The most economical XJ-S? This car has been fitted with a 2.8-litre triple-SU engine by an enthusiast.

APPENDIX A
Technical specifications

Series 1 XJ6 4.2 saloon – produced 1968 to 1973
Engine: 6-cyl, 92.7 × 106mm, 4, 235cc, CR 9:1 (8:1 alternative), twin 2in HD8 SU carbs, approx 180bhp at 5,500rpm, torque 230lb/ft at 3,500rpm.
Transmission: All-synchro 4-speed manual gearbox with 3.54:1 (later 3.31 except USA/Canada) final-drive ratio (3.77:1 with optional overdrive, giving 2.94:1 when engaged), or 3-speed Borg-Warner Model 8 (later Model 12) automatic gearbox with 3.54:1 (later 3.31 except USA/Canada) final-drive ratio.
Suspension: Front by semi-trailing double wishbones, coil springs, telescopic dampers, anti-roll bar; rear by lower wishbone/upper drive-shaft link, radius arms, twin coil-spring/damper units per side.
Steering: Rack-and-pinion, power-assisted. Brakes: Girling disc, 11.8in diameter outboard front, 10.4in inboard rear, Lockheed vacuum servo.
Wheels and tyres: 6K × 15in bolt-on pressed-steel wheels carrying Dunlop E70 205 VR-15 SP Sport radial tyres.
Dimensions: Wheelbase 9ft 0¾in; front track 4ft 10in, rear track 4ft 10½in; length 15ft 9½in; width 5ft 9¼in; height 4ft 6in.

Series 1 XJ6 2.8 saloon – produced 1968 to 1973
Engine: 6-cyl, 83 x 86mm, 2,792cc, CR 9:1 (8:1 alternative), twin 2in SU HD8 carbs, approx 150bhp at 6,000rpm.
Transmission: As for 4.2 except final-drive ratio – standard 4.27:1, overdrive 4.55:1 (giving 3.54:1 with overdrive engaged), automatic 4.27:1.

Series 1 XJ12 saloon – produced 1972 to 1973
Engine: 12-cyl, 90 × 70mm, 5,343cc, CR 9:1 (8:1), 4 Zenith 175CD SE carbs, approx 250bhp at 6,000rpm (241 at 5,750), torque 302lb/ft at 3,500 rpm (285 at 3,500).
Transmission: 3-speed automatic Borg-Warner Model 12 with 3.31:1 final-drive ratio, limited-slip differential.
Suspension and steering: As for 4.2. Brakes: Girling ventilated disc front, 11.18in diameter, non-ventilated disc rear, 10.38in diameter, Girling servo.
Wheels and tyres: 6K × 15in diameter wheels carrying steel-braced Dunlop E70 205 VR-15 SP Sport radial tyres.
Dimensions: As for 4.2 saloon.

Series 1 XJ6L 4.2 saloon – produced 1972 to 1973
As for standard 4.2 saloon except:
Wheelbase: 9ft 4¾in. Length: 16ft 2¾in.

Series 1 XJ12L – produced 1972 to 1973
As for standard XJ12 except for increased wheelbase and length in common with XJ6L.

Series 2 XJ6L 4.2 (XJ4.2 from May 1975) – produced 1973 to 1979
As for Series 1 XJ6L. Note: Standard-wheelbase Series 2 4.2 produced for one year 1973-74, specification as for standard Series 1 4.2.

Series 2 XJ12L (XJ5.3 from May 1975) – produced 1973 to 1979
As for Series 1 XJ12L (no standard-wheelbase Series 2 XJ12 made), except from May 1975 and introduction of fuel injection:
Engine (fuel-injected): 285bhp at 5,750rpm, torque 294lb/ft at 3,500rpm. Final drive 3.31:1. Note: GM 400 gearbox fitted from 1977.

XJ6C two-door coupe (XJ4.2C from May 1975) – announced 1973, produced 1975 to 1977
As for Series 2 4.2 saloon except:
Wheelbase: 9ft 1in. Length: 15ft 9½in.

XJ12C two-door coupe (XJ5.3C from May 1975) – announced 1973, produced 1975 to 1977
As for Series 2 XJ5.3 fuel-injection except:
Wheelbase: 9ft 1in. Length: 15ft 9½in.

Series 2 XJ3.4 saloon – produced 1975 to 1979
As for XJ4.2 saloon except:
Engine: 83 × 106mm, 3,442cc, CR 8.8:1, twin SU 1¾in HSC carbs, 160 bhp at 5,000rpm, torque 189lb/ft at 3,500rpm.
Transmission: Automatic Borg-Warner Model 65 3-speed gearbox with 3.54:1 final-drive ratio, or four-speed manual gearbox with 3.54:1 final-drive ratio.

Series 3 XJ4.2 saloon – produced 1979 to 1985
As for Series 2 except:
Engine: fuel-injected, CR 8.7:1 (7.8:1 USA), 200bhp at 5,000rpm (176bhp at 4,750rpm USA), torque 236lb/ft at 2,750rpm (219 at 2,500rpm USA). Note: Fuel-injected engine fitted to USA Series 2 XJ4.2 saloons from May 1978.
Transmission: Automatic Borg Warner Model 65 (later Model 66) 3 speed gearbox with 3.31:1 or 3.07:1 final-drive ratio, or 5-speed manual gearbox with 3.31:1 or 3.07:1 final-drive ratio.

Series 3 XJ3.4 saloon – produced 1979 to 1985
As for XJ3.4 Series 2 except 5-speed manual gearbox with 3.54:1 final-drive ratio optional to Borg-Warner Model 65 (later Model 66) automatic gearbox, also with 3.54:1 final drive.

Series 3 XJ5.3 saloon – produced 1979 to 1985
As for Series 2 injection 5.3 saloon except on introduction of HE cylinder head:
Engine (HE type): CR 12.5:1, 299bhp at 5,500rpm, torque 318lb/ft at 3,000rpm. Final drive: 2.88:1. Limited-slip differential.
Wheels and tyres: 6K × 15in diameter carrying Dunlop or Pirelli 215/70 VR-15 radial tyres.

XJ-S GT – produced from 1975
Engine: As for Series 2 5.3 injection saloon and Series 3 5.3 HE saloon.
Transmission: As above, except 4-speed manual gearbox available 1975-79 with 3.07:1 final-drive ratio (no overdrive offered). Final-drive ratio 2.88:1 from introduction of HE model in July 1981. Limited-slip differential.

Suspension, steering and brakes: As Series 2/Series 3 5.3 saloons.
Wheels and tyres: 6K × 15in diameter alloy wheels carrying Dunlop SP Super steel-braced 205/70 VR-15 or Pirelli P5 205 VR radials. From July 1981, 6½K × 15in diameter new-style alloy wheels carrying Dunlop or Pirelli 215/70 VR radial tyres.
Dimensions: Wheelbase 8ft 6in; front track 4ft 10½in, rear track 4ft 10in; length 15ft 11¾in; width 5ft 10½in; height 4ft 2in.

XJ-SC 3.6 Cabriolet – produced from 1983
Engine: 6-cyl, 91 × 92mm, 3,590cc, CR 9.6:1, Lucas fuel injection, installed 225bhp at 5,300rpm, torque 240lb/ft at 4,000rpm.
Transmission: Getrag 5-speed manual gearbox with 3.54:1 final-drive ratio. Limited-slip differential.
Suspension: As XJ-S HE except rear anti-roll bar 0.811mm instead of 0.875mm diameter.
Steering, brakes, wheels and tyres: As for XJ-S HE.

XJ-S 3.6 – produced from 1983
As for XJ-SC 3.6 except 6K instead of 6½K wheels.

APPENDIX B

Chassis numbers, engine numbers and vehicle identification

Chassis number sequences
Reference to these sequences should identify the type of body and engine of any vehicle from the number carried on them.

Model Series 1:	Years current	Engine no. prefix	Chassis nos. begin RHD	LHD
XJ6 4.2	Sept 68 – Jul 73	7L	1L 1001	1L 50001
XJ6 2.8	Sept 68 – Jul 73	7G	1G 1001	1G 50001
XJ6L 4.2	Oct 72 – Jul 73	7L	2E 1001	2E 50001
XJ12	Jul 72 – Aug 73	7P	1P 1001	1P 50001
XJ12L	Oct 72 – Aug 73	7P	2C 1001	2C 50001

Series 2:				
XJ6 2.8	Sept 73 – Mar 75	7G	–	2U 50001
XJ6 4.2	Sept 73 – Nov 74	7L/8L post-73	2N 1001	2N 50001
XJ6L 4.2	Sept 73 – Feb 79	7L/8L post-73	2T 1001	2T 50001
XJ12L	Sept 73 – Feb 79	7P	2R 1001	2R 50001
XJ6C	Sept 73 – Nov 77	8L	2J 1001	2J 50001
XJ12C	Sept 73 – Nov 77	7P	2G 1001	2G 50001
XJ 3.4	Apr 75 – Feb 79	8A	3A 1001	3A 50001

Note: From May 1978, and thus during S2 production, Vehicle

Identification Numbers replaced chassis numbers. Final conventional S2 numbers were:
XJ 3.4	3A.6004	3A.51486
XJ 4.2	2T.27236	2T.74576
XJ 5.3	2R.5157	2R.60069
XJ-S	2W.5000	2W.55915

Series 3:
Note: See below for model identification code.
Model	Years current	Engine no. prefix	Chassis nos. begin
XJ 3.4	Mar 79 –	8A	100781
XJ 4.2	Mar 79 –	8L	300003 (300009 auto)
XJ 5.3	Mar 79 –	7P	101140
Sov. 4.2	Sept 83 –	8L	370502
Sov. 5.3	Sept 83 –	7P	370548

XJ-S:
XJ-S GT	Sept 75 – Jun 81	8S	2W.1001	2W.50001
XJ-S HE	Jul 81 –	8S		
XJ-S 3.6FHC	Oct 83 –		112586	
XJ-S 3.6 Cab	Oct 83 –		112588	

Vehicle Identification Numbers

The table below identifies the S3 and XJ-S model range; for interest, Daimler models are also included.

Jaguar

Model	Engine	Class	Transmission	Stg.	VIN Prefix code
XJ6	3.4		Automatic	RHD	JAALA3CC
XJ6	3.4		Automatic	LHD	JAALA4CC
XJ6	3.4		Manual 5 speed	RHD	JAALA7CC
XJ6	3.4		Manual 5 speed	LHD	JAALA8CC
XJ6	4.2		Automatic	RHD	JAALP3CC
XJ6	4.2		Automatic	LHD	JAALP4CC
XJ6	4.2		Manual	RHD	JAALP7CC
XJ6	4.2		Manual	LHD	JAALP8CC
XJ6	4.2	N.A.S. 1979	Automatic	LHD	JAVLN49C
XJ6	4.2	Australian	Automatic	RHD	JAALR3CC
XJ6	4.2	Swedish	Automatic	LHD	JAALR4CC
XJ6	4.2	Japanese	Automatic	RHD	JAJLN3CC
XJ6	4.2	Japanese	Automatic	LHD	JAJLN4CC
XJ12	5.3		Automatic	RHD	JBALW3CC
XJ12	5.3		Automatic	LHD	JBALW4CC
XJ12	5.3	N.A.S 1979	Automatic	LHD	JBVLV49C
XJ12	5.3	Australian	Automatic	RHD	JBALY3CC
XJ12	5.3	Japanese	Automatic	RHD	JBJLV3CC
XJ12	5.3	Japanese	Automatic	LHD	JBJLV4CC
XJ12	5.3	California '79	Automatic	LHD	JBVLX49C
XJ6	4.2 Sov.		Automatic	RHD	JCALP
XJ12	5.3 Sov.		Automatic	RHD	JBALW
XJ-S	5.3		Manual	RHD	JNUEW3ACB
XJ-S	5.3		Automatic	RHD	JNUEW3AC
XJ-S	3.6		Manual	RHD	JNAEC

Daimler

Model	Engine	Class	Transmission	Stg.	VIN Prefix code
Sovereign	3.4		Automatic	RHD	DCALA3CC
Sovereign	3.4		Automatic	LHD	DCALA4CC
Sovereign	3.4		Manual 5 speed	RHD	DCALA7CC
Sovereign	3.4		Manual 5 speed	LHD	DCALA8CC
Sovereign	4.2		Automatic	RHD	DCALP3CC
Sovereign	4.2		Automatic	LHD	DCALP4CC
Sovereign	4.2		Manual 5 speed	RHD	DCALP7CC
Sovereign	4.2		Manual 5 speed	LHD	DCALP8CC
Sovereign	4.2	Australian	Automatic	RHD	DCALR3CC
Vanden Plas	4.2		Automatic	RHD	DCRLP3CC
Vanden Plas	4.2		Automatic	LHD	DCRLP4CC
Vanden Plas	4.2	Australian	Automatic	RHD	DCRLR3CC
Double-Six	5.3		Automatic	RHD	DDALW3CC
Double-Six	5.3		Automatic	LHD	DDALW4CC
Double-Six	5.3	Australian	Automatic	RHD	DDALY3CC
Double-Six VDP	5.3		Automatic	RHD	DDRLW3CC
Double-Six VDP	5.3		Automatic	LHD	DDRLW4CC
Double-Six VDP	5.3	Australian	Automatic	RHD	DDRLY3CC
Double-Six VDP	5.3	Japanese	Automatic	RHD	DDRLV3CC

APPENDIX C

Production changes by date, chassis and engine number

Below are listed some major specification changes to the XJ series by date, chassis and engine number; dates refer mainly to when dealers were informed of changes. In some cases, cars prior to the date given may have been given the new parts. Up to May 1978 chassis numbers incorporating a single letter and different numbering for right-hand and left-hand-drive cars were used; after that date Vehicle Identification Numbers (VIN) were employed which use multi-letter coding.

See Appendix B for an explanation of these and engine prefixes.

All numbers given are those from which a specification change began.

Engine and transmission

Series 1

May 69   2.8-litre cam covers secured at front centre position by countersunk screw: 7G.1638.

June 69   Cylinder block drain tap replaced by plug.

Aug 69   Flexible mounting of carbs to manifold (similar to 420G): 2.8 7G.3146, 4.2 7L.5176.

Oct 69   Improved rear engine mounting on manual cars. 2.8-litre: inlet manifold shortened at front to provide better access to distributor; also extended thermostat housing: 7G.5021.

Nov 69   New camshafts with redesigned profiles to give quieter operation and longer periods between tappet adjustment: 2.8 7G.5795, 4.2 7L.8344.

Jan 70   Exhaust emission cam covers drilled and tapped for warm air duct; alternator guard fitted: 2.8 7G.0125, 4.2 7L.0644.

Mar 70   Emission-type exhaust manifold standardized on all cars; 2.8 7G.6479, 4.2 7L.9107. Air conditioning fan cowl standardized on all cars.

June 70   New oil sump strainer to overcome cavitation which might occur with sudden reduction in engine speed: 2.8 7G.8383, 4.2 7L.12104.

June 70   Model 12 automatic gearbox (with D-2-1 selector) replaced Model 8 on 4.2 cars: IL.4988/IL.53343. Revised pistons for 2.8-litre: 7G.8849.

Oct 70   8:1 instead of 9:1 CR for USA/Canada 4.2-litre: 1L.55686. Improved rear engine mounting. 'Otter' thermostat controlling automatic choke replaced earlier type; 2.8 7G.12062, 4.2 7L.18345. Revised exhaust camshafts without drilling in back of cams fitted to reduce oil consumption; 2.8 7G.12116, 4.2 7L.18528. Improved Model 35 automatic gearbox fitted to 2.8-litre.

Dec 70   Modified oil delivery pipe fixing to pump to prevent vibration damage to brazed joint at flange; 2.8 7G.13125. Introduction of suffix letters to denote compression ratio: 'H' high, 'S' standard, 'L' low. Fuel line filter now in spare wheel compartment. Revised camshaft sprocket adjuster plate due to lobe- type plate (fitted in place of original vernier-teeth type) breaking away from camshaft flange. 2.8 7G.7063, 4.2 7L.9722. (suspect plate fitted from 7G.5226 and 7L.6878 to above numbers).

Mar 71   SU HS8 carbs fitted with automatic enriching device (AED) for easier starting and improved warm-up on 4.2-litre: 7L.26489.

Apr 71   Improved crankshaft rear oil seal. 2.8 7G.16033. Automatic cars given modified accelerator cable and new kickdown switch.

Dec 71   Modified clutch assembly fitted to all cars.

Mar 72   2.8 engine number relocated on RH side of cylinder block flywheel housing flange: 7G.19023. 2.8-litre given 4.2-type oil sump assembly. 13lb radiator cap fitted to all non-air conditioned cars.

May 72   New starter and relay cable fitted to 4.2: 7L.49859.

June 72   Alternator (18 ACR) commonized with air conditioned cars (including control box, ignition warning light control formerly behind LH facia panel). Width of 2.8-litre centre main bearing reduced to allow use of two standard-size instead of oversize thrust washers: 7G.21017.

July 72   Recommendation for static ignition timing on 2.8-litre to be set at 6 degrees BTDC to provide greater margin relative to onset of detonation at wide throttle openings.

Aug 72   Printed circuit ballast resistor introduced on XJ12: 7P.1616.

Oct 72   N9Y instead of N10Y spark plugs specified for XJ12. Deletion of small-end oil feed drilling from con-rod on XJ12: 7P.1985.

Dec 72   Revised bearing with improved linining material for XJ12: 7P.2144.

Jan 73   New gearbox countershaft needle-roller bearings: KFN.19993.

Feb 73   Revised inlet/exhaust camshafts for 2.8 and 4.2 engines, identified by absence of groove on periphery of cam flange, end sealed by plug. 2.8 7G.23362, 4.2 7L.64860.

Mar 73   Crankshaft rear oil seal standardized with V12; 2.8 7G.23781, 4.2 7L.67336. Improved valve guides.

May 73   Additional vacuum brake take-off from RH inlet manifold on V12 for increased low-speed assistance.

July 73   Improved oil pump housing on V12: 7P.4469. Oil capacity increased by 3 pints to 19 pints on V12 to reduce possible oil surge in extreme conditions (new dipstick identified by blue plastic insert): 7P.9469. Improved heat dissipation exhaust valve guide inserts on 4.2-litre: 7L.73778.

Series 2

Oct 73   Modified camshaft with revised cam profile, USA/Canada V12. Modified synchro operating sleeve to prevent jumping out of forward gears on 4.2: 7L.74881.

Dec 73   Model 65 automatic gearbox fitted to 4.2: 2N.2716/51630, 6L 2T.1423/50002 (air conditioned XJ6 USA/Canada 2N.52204).

Feb 74   High-load coil and amplifier on 12L: 7P.8169.

Mar 74   Revised exhaust gas recirculation system on USA cars: 2N.53480.

Aug 74   V12-type oil filler cap fitted to 6-cyl cars (with appropriately modified cam cover): 2.8 7G.25130, 4.2 7L.96758.

Oct 74   New 4.2 con-rod with plain tapered shank (no rib): 8L.5028.

Nov 74   Revised cam corner seal on 4.2 as on V12: 8L:9081. Revised valve tappets: V12 7P.10087, 4.2 8L.11129.

Jan 75   Revised oil drilling with only one oil feed per journal, 4.2 8L.13995.

Jan 75   Phased introduction of electric fuel injection (EFI) on V12 cars: North America only: XJ12L 2R.53945, XJ12C 2G.50001 (except 047-54). Elsewhere XJ5.3 2R.3923/53903, XJ5.3C 2G.1015/50037. Stainless steel front and rear silencers fitted in place of aluminized on 6 and 12-cyl cars. Plastic cover for coil, 4.2 8L.11781. 1975 model year changes began: 4.2 2T.121151/55047 (USA 2T.54779), XJ12L 2R.3923/53903 (engine number 7P.25001), XJ12C 2G.1015/50037 (50001 USA), same engine number. Note: These changes coincided with introduction of EFI on V12 cars.

          Revised panel and console switches deleting outer silver lines from switch body: 3.4 3A.1948/50494, 6L 2T.13541/50418, 12L 2R.3936/54215, 12C 2G.1097/50421.

May 75   Revised rear main bearing side seal introduced on V12 for improved seal between bearing cap and block. Anti run-on solenoid fitted to 3.4-litre.

Dec 75   Water pump and pulley, torquatrol unit standardized with V12: 3.4 8A.3991, 4.2 8L.25469.

Jan 76   1976 model year changes began: 3.4 3A.2681/50666, 6L 2T.150261/58224, 6C 2J.1774/51946.

Feb 76   Disposable cannister-type element oil filter assembly introduced on non-oil-cooler cars: 3.4 8A.4596, 4.2 8L.28179. XJ-S type fuel pump standardized on all V12 cars.

May 76   50,000-mile instead of 25,000-mile exhaust catalyst unit introduced on California cars: 6L 2T.60545, 6C 2J.52414.

June 76   Introduction of USA-specification engines and associated equipment on cars for Sweden and Australia. New carburettors and inlet manifold fitted on 3.4: 3A.3155/50776.

July 76   50,000-mile exhaust catalyst unit fitted to V12 cars. USA-specification engines adopted for Japan.

Oct 76   New and improved EFI equipment for V12 cars including cold-start injectors, thermo-time switch, pressure sensor, distributor, power amplifier, control unit, etc: 12L 2R.4194/56722, 12C 2G.1272/51080, XJ-S 2W.2030/52556.

Nov 76   2-piece fan cowl assembly suitable for all air-conditioned 6-cyl models introduced. 25 ACR alternator replaced 20 ACR unit on air conditioned models (non-air conditioned cars continued with 18 ACR).

Dec 76   Revised EFI control unit, V12 models.

Jan 77   Revised crankshaft front oil seal, 6-cyl cars.

Apr 77   Introduction of GM 400 transmission on XJ-S, from engine number 8S.7017, 2W.2833/53507 (2W.53539 USA/Canada).

Nov 77   Revised selector shafts and finger on manual transmission: 3.4 8A.8821, 4.2 8L.52217, XJ-S 8S.8632.

Jan 78   1978 model year changes began: 6L 2T.22973/68827, 12L 2R.4694/58346 (38421 USA/Canada).

Feb 78   Fuel injection 4.2 engine introduced for USA only: 2T.69451. Revised oil filter assembly with horizontal element cannister instead of vertical, 6-cyl cars: 3.4 8A.9041, 4.2 carburettor 8L.55927, 4.2 injection 8L.50476.

Mar 78   Revised exhaust system for 6-cyl cars using V12-type rear silencers and tailpipes: 3.4 3A.5181/51486, 6L 2T.23400/69164, 6C 2J.3605/53897.

May 78   New torque convertor with ribbed impeller blades for 6-cyl saloons: 8L.65761. Announcement of 5-speed gearbox for XJ6L. Introduction of VIN system for numbering models.

Oct 78   5-speed gearbox introduced: 3.4 6L. VIN 100781, engine numbers 3.4 8A.10091, 4.2 8L.67950. Revised front downpipe and exhaust manifold with 2-bolt instead of 4-bolt fixing: 3.4 3A.5918, 6L 2T.26733. Revised radiator assembly 3.4 and 6L, VIN 104176. Tie bracket fitted between engine sump and torque converter housing, automatic cars: VIN 104238. New distributor and resiting of ignition amplifier from engine to front crossmember: 12L 7P.37048, XJ-S 8S.11262. Increased interference fit of valve seats following isolated reports of loosening.

Nov 78   Introduction of EFI 4.2 engine to Japan: 2T.73490.

Dec 78   New water pump assembly incorporating single instead of double groove pulley.

Feb 79   New radiator assembly, S2 saloons: 110552. Revised flywheel and drive plate assembly deleting need for locating dowels, 3.4 and 4.2 cars.

Apr 79   XJ-S 1979 model year changes began VIN 10855 (101878 California).

Series 3

June 79   Introduction of Model 66 Borg-Warner gearbox for S3 6-cyl models: 3.4 8A.10747, 4.2 8L.82730.

Aug 79   Reversion to original flywheel C.32352 from lightweight flywheel EAC2230, all S2 and S3 6-cyl saloons, due to problems experienced with the latter.

Oct 79   Revised reverse gear idler incorporating plain bush instead of needle roller bearings on 3.4 and 4.2-litre manual cars.

Dec 79   New 'slotted deck' 4.2-litre cylinder block, head and gasket introduced (new block requires new or modified old head – 8 new water holes drilled; new gasket all-time replacement, but essential for new head and block). Revised petrol pump mounting for XJ-S: VIN 103407.

Jan 80   New water pump incorporating ball/roller bearing and spindle assembly, S3 6-cyl saloons: 3.4 8A.11232, 4.2 8L.88583.

Nov 80   Oil sump drain plug moved to allow draining without removing ancillary parts, e.g. grass shields, V12 models: Saloon 7P.43003, XJ-S 8S.17191. Introduction of P-jetronic EFI on V12 models: Saloon VIN 310613, XJ-S 104146.

Jan 81   1981 model year changes to XJ6 4.2 began for North America at VIN 320092 California, 321108 USA, 322541 Canada.

Chassis
Series 1

Jan 69   3.31 final-drive ratio replaced 3.54 on all automatic cars except USA/Canada on XJ6 4.2: 1L.1324/50209. On 2.8 cars, 4.09 replaced 4.27 ratio: 1G.1095/50066. Note: All standard-transmission 4.2 cars were fitted from inception with 3.31, contrary to owner's handbook.

Mar 69   Revised anti-roll bar and mountings, 2.8-litre: 1G.1098/50066, 4.2 1L.1371/50253.

May 69   Modified front spring pans to provide adequate clearance for front tyres: 2.8 1G.1530/50236, 4.2 1L.2125/50736. Stiffer range of front springs, 4.2-litre: 1L.2671/51097. Handbrake control modified to conform with brake already fitted on German, Swiss and Swedish cars.

June 69   Stiffer front spring fitted to 2.8-litre cars: 1G.1733/50369.

139

July 69	New brake fluid reservoir on inboard, not rear, of booster.
May 70	3.07 final-drive replaced 3.31 on automatic 4.2-litre cars for Europe (most), Australia, New Zealand and Africa.
Aug 70	Additional front disc brake shields fitted for protection of pads. Modified rear hubs with integral wheel location spigot.
May 72	New type of brake servo non-return valve fitted (in vacuum hose inlet instead of brake servo casing).
Aug 72	Slotted brake pads introduced to assit bedding-in.
Dec 72	Modified steering pinion valve assembly on rack and pinion due to isolated cases of self-steer: 2.8 1G.12876/55876, 4.2 IL.28582/69099.
Jan 73	Revised rack and pinion assembly on all cars.
June 73	Phosphor bronze replaced steel rear hub spacer to prevent 'click'.

Series 2

Jan 74	Revised braking system with new master cylinder and four-piston front caliper: 4.2 2N.3480/51655, 6L 2T.1526/50002, 2.8 2U.50002, 12L 2R.1478/50211.
Nov 74	Revised final-drive outboard shaft and bearings, taper-roller, not ball, on 6 and 12-cyl cars.
Jan 75	1975 model year changes began: 6L 4.2-litre: 2T.12115/55047 (USA 54779); for V12 cars see under May 1975.
Apr 75	Alloy road wheels introduced for V12 EFI models only (Note: These will foul calipers on other models.)
May 75	Revised steering rack with 8-tooth pinion fitted to improve handling of V12 EFI car, together with revised anti-roll bar, new vertical link assembly, new steering arms, revised upper wishbones and different castor angle: 12L 7P.25001, 2R.3923/53903 (USA 53945); 12C 7P.25001, 2G.1015/50037 (USA 50001).
June 75	Revised speedometer cable and extended angle drive at speedo head.
Sept 75	Revised tandem prop-shaft assembly and centre bearing mounting, 6-cyl cars.
Nov 75	Front calipers of 6-cyl cars revised to commonize with V12 cars fitted with alloy wheels (so can now accept latter without fouling): 3.4 3A.23061/50637, 6L 2T.14089/57185, 6C 2J.1601/51519.
Jan 76	1976 model year changes began on 6-cyl cars (except USA/Australia/Canada/Japan/Sweden): 3.4 3A.2681/50666, 6L 2T.150261/50224 (USA 56746), 6C 2J.1774/51946 (USA 51369).
Mar 77	Introduction of new alloy road wheels (except XJ-S) also as optional equipment. Note: For S2 cars, new and existing wheels interchangeable, but S1 cars must be fitted with new wheel CAC 1701 only.
May 77	Revised brake booster and master cylinder fitted with fluid

	reservoir attached direct to master cylinder (except Scandinavia).
June 77	Batch introduction of Alford & Alder rack-and-pinion assembly (also Nov 76 and Oct 77), replacing Adwest assembly. Identified by central porting ring which accepts hydraulic pipe (absent on Adwest).
Jan 78	Revised wheel nuts for alloy wheel with 7/8in instead of 3/4in flats and non-mulled shoulder (requires new wheelbrace). 1978 model year changes on XJ-S began: 2W.4023/54660 (USA 54673). For saloons: 6L 2T.22973/68827, V12 2R.4694/58346 (USA 58421).
May 78	Final batch of revised rack and pinion.
Nov 78	Alford and Alder rack-and-pinion standardized.

Series 3

Jan 80	Improved GM400 torque converter, V12 models: Saloons 7P.42300, XJ-S 8S.16461.
May 80	Modified steering rack assembly with metric pressure pipe connections to prevent leakage and improve driver feel in straight-ahead position (longer pinion), including new Saginaw pump. Known as 1980 PTFE unit. VIN 313365.
July 80	New brake disc of improved material to minimize brake judder.

Body, fixtures and fittings
Series 1

Mar 69	Panel light fuse introduced.
Apr 69	Provision made for fitting inertia-reel seat belts (except USA/Canada).
Aug 69	Mud flaps offered as option. Provision made for fitting head restraints: 2.8 1G.2343/50777, 4.2 1L.3404/51596.
Nov 69	Exhaust heat shield fitted under passenger compartment floor: 2.8 1G.3765/51720, 4.2 1L.4764/52684.
Jan 70	Load-shedding ignition switch fitted.
Mar 70	Revised windscreen and backlight rubbers. Bolt-on instead of spot-welds for bonnet lock control cable bracket attached to wing valance channels; kit to adapt earlier cars offered. Side/flasher lights altered to ECE requirements.
Apr 70	Improved door locks fitted to prevent straining of linkage if interior remote control operated to full extent when child locks on. Scuttle vent grille changed to satin chrome from bright chrome to prevent glare: 2.8 1G.5271/52459, 4.2 1L.7452/53778. Revised demister vent-fitted to eliminate distortion in high temperatures: 2.8 1G.5300/52604, 4.2 1L.7643/53972.
May 70	New interior mirror fitted. 2.8 given same petrol pumps (AUF

301) as 4.2: 1G.5274/52465. Revised spare wheel cover, tool roll and jack stowage (removed from spare wheel compartment to luggage compartment): 2.8 1G.5781/52901, 4.2 1L.8667/54497. Modified window regulators fitted.

Aug 70 Stop and tail lights with lens to European regulations. Expanded aluminium mesh filter added to scuttle vent grille.

Oct 70 Modified front wheelarch flanges to overcome tyre fouling: 2.8 1G.4559/52019, 4.2 1L.5687/53100. New door tread plates incorporating name 'Jaguar' fitted: 2.8 1G.6820/53465, 4.2 1L.10195/55487. Non-reflective instrument bezels and water gauge with revised markings and 100lb instead of 60lb oil pressure gauge fitted: 2.8 1G.7415/53726, 4.2 1L.11114/56177. 'Hot line' heated rear window with visible element in toughened not laminated glass backlight fitted.

Mar 71 3-piece rear bumper introduced: 2.8 1G.8194/54708, 4.2 1L.13172/58287. Modified stop and tail lights fitted with longer reversing lights and reflector now below. Fresh-air ventilation to footwells via intake under outer headlamp rim.

Apr 71 Revised cigar lighter fitted.

Nov 71 New disc-type door locks (keyless locking now impossible): 2.8 1G.10713/55640, 4.2 1L.20648/63862.

Mar 72 Seat belt alarm fitted USA/Canada 4.2-litre cars: 1L.64775. Standard 2.8-litre saloon discontinued.

May 72 Waso instead of Britax steering column lock fitted.

June 72 Relocation of chassis numbers from left-hand to right-hand wing valance: 2.8 1G.12499/55801, 4.2 1L.27654/67384.

Aug 72 Ballast resistor incorporating printed circuit introduced on XJ12: 7P.1616.

Nov 72 Fuel pump cut-out inertia switch fitted: 4.2: 2N.3205/51656, 4.2 6L 2T.1477/50002, 2.8 2U.50002, XJ12L 2R.1343/50219.

Jan 73 Frigidaire compressor fitted to XJ6 air-conditioned cars: 7L.58469.

Feb 73 Fuse rating for heated backlight raised from 15 to 25 amps. Revised method of mounting fuel pumps using foam cushion, plastic cradle and rubber retaining straps, XJ12: 1P.1323/50394.

Mar 73 Chassis numbers on all saloon cars now relocated on extension of right-hand wing valance stay bracket.

May 73 New steering column lock fitted.

Series 2

Nov 70 Heat shield installed over panel light rheostat to prevent possible damage to wiring harness. Bracket introduced to retain fuel cut-out inertia switch.

Jan 74 Revised harness to fuel gauge fitted.

Mar 74 Grommeted holes introduced in front valance of XJ12L to allow direct access to oil cooler mounting screws.

Oct 74 Revised bonnet stay incorporating check arm fitted.

Nov 74 Front bumper underrider modified with revised method of attaching to body, 6L and 12L.

Mar 75 1975 model year changes began: 6L 2T.12279/55061 (USA 54779), 12L 2R.3923/53903 (USA 53945), 12C 2G.1015/50037 (USA 50001). Included bumper beam and blades, side/flasher lights USA. New speedometer introduced.

Aug 75 Revised panel and control switches deleting outer silver line from switch body: 3.4 3A.1948/50494, 6L 2T.13541/56416, 12L 2R.3939/54215, 12C 2G.10971/50421.

Jan 76 1976 new model year changes began for 3.4: 3A.2681/50666, 6L 2T.15026/58224, 6C 2J.1774/51946.

Feb 76 Revised door trim with more secure fitting to door shell, XJ-S.

June 76 New instrument pack, oil pressure indicator and transmitter, XJ-S: mph cars 2W.1649/51882, kph cars 2W.1550/51731.

July 76 Rationalization by Lucas of front side/flasher lamps, all cars except XJ-S.

Jan 77 New door glass tensioner and regulator to give improved window lift, XJ coupe: 6C 2J.2574/52933, 12C 2G.1340/51117.

Dec 77 Revised quartz halogen lights outer assembly, flatter and with 'E' mark, available as option on all S2 models.

Feb 78 Revised instruments, warning light clusters, facia central outlet grille and outer vent assemblies; new parts have matt black surrounds instead satin chrome: 3.4 3A.5100/51449, 6L 2T.22883/68745 (USA 69451), 6C 2J.3452/53823, 12L 2R.4690/58295, 12C 2G.1539/51257. Piloted headlights (*e.g.* with integral sidelights) and new front flasher lamps with all-amber lens: 3.4 3A.5124/51475, 6L 2T.22968/68818, 6C 2J.3487/53852, 12L 2R.4694/58346, 12C 2G. 1555/51259. XJ-S update including revised horns, stop/tail/flasher lamps, 'B' post finishers and remote-control door mirrors.

Mar 78 Quartz halogen headlights standard on 4.2 6L and 12L (GB and certain other countries, not USA). 1978 model year changes began: 6L 2T.22973/68827, 12L 2R.4694/58346 (38421 USA).

Apr 78 Stainless-steel drip moulding finishers for painted-roof cars only: 3.4 3A.5165/51485, 6L 2T.23258/69031, 12L 2R.58462.

May 78 Revised front doors, all four-door saloons with electric windows.

June 78 Revised rear quarter-panel trim moulding for vinyl-roof models, 6L, 12L, but not Vanden Plas.

Sept 78 Re-introduction of adjustable-type demister vent assemblies, replacing fixed vane-type on facia pad top, Hong Kong only.

Oct 78 Revised remote-control door handles and mechanism. New flasher side repeater light, Italy only. XLS leather-covered steering wheel C.44645 introduced progressively in place of non-leather type C.38614 on saloons: VIN 105679.

Dec 78 Revised windscreen rubber giving improved retention. New condenser assembly fitted to air-conditioned 6-cyl cars: VIN

107661. Leather-covered steering wheel (XJ-S type) fitted to S2 range: VIN 106276.

Jan 79 Lighting switch with symbol introduced on S2 saloons: VIN 108486. Instrument pack assembly including dual-calibrated speedometer (mph and kph) and rev-counter fitted to XJ-S: GB, VIN 101179, USA, VIN 101318.

Series 3

July 79 New outboard halogen lights including H4 flat lens with improved thermal shock reistance fitted to S3 saloons without headlight wash/wipe: VIN 302037 (302954 France). New lockable fuel filler cap fitted to XJ-S, VIN 102741.

Sept 79 New low-profile aerial on RH wing, S3 saloons (not Germany or Japan). New handbrake assembly, XJ-S.

Oct 79 Batch of non-metallic dark green cellulose low-bake paint instead of thermoplastic acrylic.

Jan 80 Fog guard lamps standardized on XJ-S, UK/Eire: VIN 103476. 85mph speedometer fitted, USA cars only, XJ-S: VIN 103813. Windscreen washer jet assembly polished instead of matt chrome, saloons: VIN 309048.

Feb 80 Manually operated temperature override to control face – level outlets (thumb wheel under radio space), saloons: RHD 310613, LHD 310676.

May 80 New panel light control giving minimum brightness at 'stop' position instead of 'off'.

Aug 80 Symbol-type minor instruments fitted to all mph-speedometer cars except for USA: 4.2 saloons VIN 316068, 5.3 saloons 316197.

Nov 80 New steering column switch gear assemblies with modified arm crank, S3 saloons: VIN 313771 speed-control cars, 315383 others. Bonnet liners replace sprayed-on Aquplas: S3 6-cyl: VIN 314014, 12-cyl VIN 313707.

APPENDIX D

Production figures and prices on introduction

Note: Price of cheapest model available is given.

Model	Price	RHD	LHD	Total
Series 1:				
XJ6 4.2	£2,254	33,467	25,505	58,972
XJ6 2.8	£1,897	13,301	6,125	19,426
XJ6L 4.2	£3,464	583	1	584
XJ12	£3,726	720	1,762	2,482
XJ12L	£4,052	750	3	753
Series 2:*				
XJ6 4.2	£3,674	7,463	4,907	12,370
XJ6L 4.2	£4,124	26,236	24,676	50,912
XJ12L	£4,702	4,157	10,069	14,226
XJ6C	£4,260	2,606	3,899	6,505
XJ12C	£5,181	604	1,269	1,873
XJ6 3.4	£4,795	5,004	1,486	6,490

Model	Price	Total
Series 3: **		
XJ6 4.2	£12,326	61,089
XJ6 3.4	£11,189	4,446
XJ12	£15,014	1,911
XJ12 HE	£18,209	947
XJ12 Sov HE	£20,955	3,117
XJ6 Sov	£18,495	(included in XJ6 4.2)
XJ-S	£8,900	14,972
XJ-S HE	£18,950	13,729
XJ-S 3.6	£19,249	524
XJ-SC 3.6	£20,756	366

*S2 production figures for 4-door models are as at May 1978 (on introduction of VIN numbers).

**S3 production figures are as at September 21, 1984. Individual totals of RHD and LHD cars not available.

How fast? How economical? How heavy?

```
*  = automatic
†  = UK spec.
( )= US emission spec.
```

	S1 4.2		2.8	S1 XJ12		S2 4.2L	S2 3.4	S2 5.3 (P.1.)		S2 5.3C	
Mean maximum speed (mph)	124/120		117/113	138	(130)	118*†	114	147	(128)	147	(128)
Acceleration (sec)											
0-30	3.1/3.9	(4.1)*	3.8/3.9	3.1	(3.1)	4.0	4.0	3.3	(3.8)	3.2	(3.3)
0-40	4.6/5.5	(5.7)	6.0/7.2	4.4	(4.3)	5.6	6.1	4.8	–	4.4	(5.3)
0-50	6.6/7.6	(8.0)	8.2/9.3	5.9	(5.7)	7.8	8.2	6.0	(6.8)	6.9	(6.6)
0-60	8.8/10.1	(10.7)	11.0/12.6	7.4	(7.7)	10.6	11.2	7.8	(8.8)	7.6	(8.2)
0-70	11.3/13.4	(14.4)	15.2/16.3	9.6	(9.8)	13.8	15.0	9.7	–	9.4	(10.7)
0-80	14.7/17.8	(19.5)	19.3/21.8	12.2	(12.6)	17.9	19.6	12.6	(14.2)	11.8	(13.0)
0-90	18.8/23.0	(–)	26.4/29.9	15.2	(16.5)	23.4	26.5	15.7	–	14.4	–
0-100	24.1/30.4	(34.1)	35.0/39.9	19.0	(24.4)	31.0	36.6	18.8	(23.5)	18.4	–
0-110	–	–	–	23.9		–	–	24.0	–	23.0	–
0-120	–	–	–	31.0	–	–	–	31.2	–	30.5	–
0-130	–	–	–	–	–	–	–	42.9	–	–	–
Standing ¼-mile	16.5/17.5	(16.0)	18.1/19.2	15.7	(16.0)	17.6	18.0	15.7	(17.0)	15.7	(16.2)
Direct top gear											
10-30	–		8.7				–				
20-40	6.3		8.7				9.6				
30-50	6.5		8.7				9.2				
40-60	6.4		8.7				9.8				
50-70	5.9		8.9				10.1				
60-80	6.8		9.8				10.9				
70-90	7.6		11.6				12.5				
80-100	9.0		14.9				16.6				
90-110	–		–				–				
Final drive ratio	3.77/3.31	(3.54)	4.55/4.09	3.31	(3.31)	3.54	3.54	3.07	(3.31)	3.31	(3.31)
Overall mpg	15.9/15.2	(15)	17/16	11,4	(10.0)	14.5	20	13.0	(13.0)	13.0	(13.0)
Kerb weight (cwt)	33/33	(33)	02½cwt	35		36	33	07	(27)	26	(36 0)

Note: First column of figures refer to UK-specification cars, manual/automatic.

	S3 4.2		S3 XJ12 HE	XJ-S GT		XJ-S HE		XJ-S 3.6
Mean maximum speed (mph)	128/120	(118)	146	153/142	(137)	153/(140)		141
Acceleration (sec)								
0-30	2.8/4.2	(4.0)	3.4	2.8/3.2	(3.8)	3.3	(3.4)	2.6
0-40	4.2/5.9	–	4.9	3.8/4.5	(5.2)	4.6		4.1
0-50	6.3/7.7	(7.9)	6.5	5.1/5.9	(6.7)	6.1	(6.3)	5.6
0-60	8.6/10.5	(10.6)	8.1	6.7/7.5	(8.6)	7.5	(8.2)	7.4
0-70	12.1/13.5	(14.3)	10.1	8.4/9.5	(11.0)	9.2	(10.5)	9.9
0-80	15.6/16.9	(19.0)	12.7	10.5/11.9	(13.9)	11.3	(13.5)	12.4
0-90	20.2/21.6	(26.0)	15.5	13.4/14.7	(–)	14.0	–	15.3
0-100	26.5/28.4	–	19.0	16.2/18.4	(22.2)	16.8	(21.3)	19.7
0-110	34.6/38.1	–	24.3	20.2/23.1	–	20.6	–	24.6
0-120	45.6/–	–	32.6	25.8/30.4	–	26.6	–	31.8
0-130	– –	–	–	– –	–	–	–	–
Standing ¼-mile	17.2/17.6	(18.2)	15.9	15.0/15.7	(16.5)	15.6	(16.3)	15.9
Direct top gear								
10-30	10.3/6.8	(5th/4th)		7.5				12.7/8.2 (5th/4th)
20-40	9.8/6.6			6.8				11.7/7.3
30-50	9.8/7.0			6.6				10.6/6.7
40-60	9.9/7.4			6.8				10.6/6.9
50-70	10.8/7.7			6.9				11.6/7.2
60-80	12.4/8.2			7.1				12.5/7.3
70-90	14.5/8.8			7.2				13.9/7.1
80-100	15.4/10.3			8.0				15.5/7.3
90-110	21.6/13.6			8.6				16.5/8.8
100-120	– /16.6			10.3				19.0/11.6
Final drive ratio	3.31/3.07	(3.07)	2.88	3.07/3.07	(3.31)	2.88	(2.88)	3.54
Overall mpg	18.3/15.7	(15.0)	16	14/14		16.3	(14.5)	17.6
Kerb weight (cwt)	34½/35	(35)	37.8	34/34	(34)	34	(34.0)	32

144